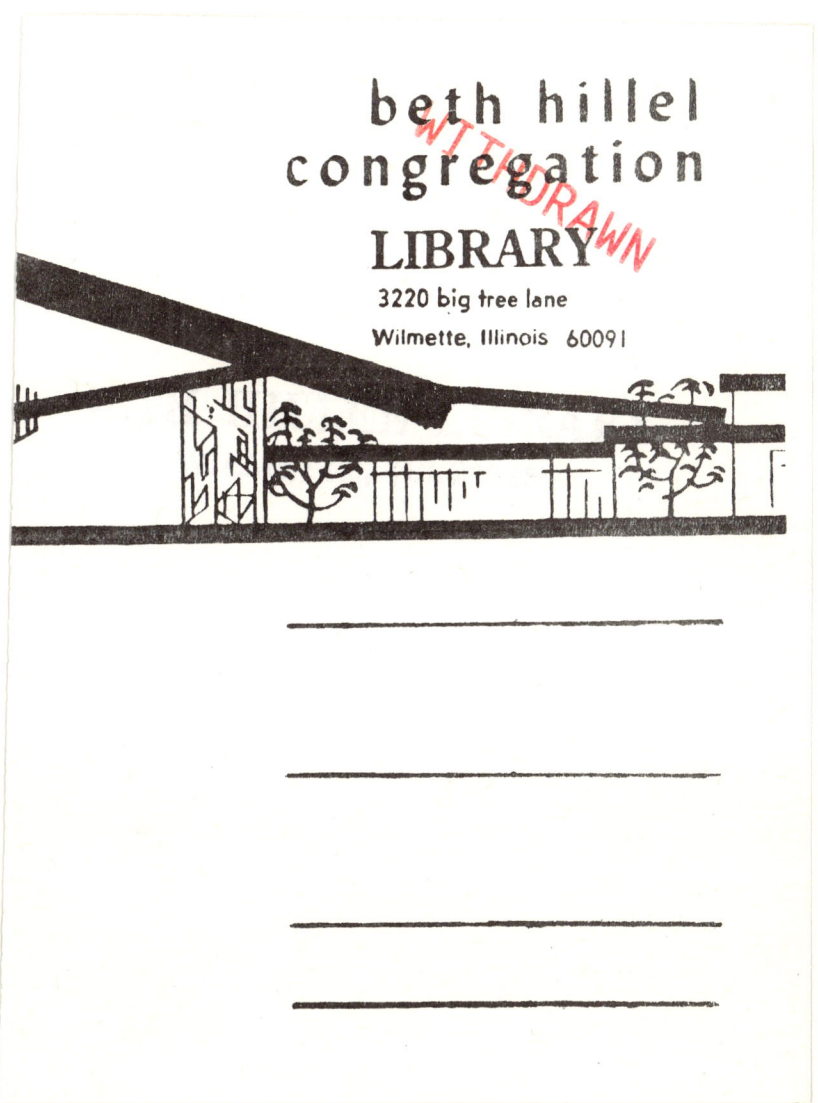

HANUKKAH CRAFTS

HANUKKAH CRAFTS

by Joyce Becker

A BONIM ACTIVITY BOOK
BONIM BOOKS

New York • London

To my husband, children, and mother
with heartfelt gratitude
and
To the memory of my father and grandmother.

J.B.

Copyright © 1978 by Joyce Becker

All rights reserved. No part of this publication may be reproduced, stored in a retrieval system, or transmitted, in any form or by any means, electronic, mechanical, photocopying, recording, or otherwise, without permission in writing from the publisher.

Library of Congress Cataloging in Publication Data

Becker, Joyce.
    Hanukkah crafts.

    (A Bonim activity book)
    Includes index.
    1. Jewish crafts. 2. Hanukkah (Feast of Lights).
I. Title.
BM729.H35B4   745.5   78-16744
ISBN 0-88482-763-1
ISBN 0-88482-765-8 pbk.

A BONIM ACTIVITY BOOK

Series Editor: Deborah Brodie
Text design by Publishing Synthesis, Ltd.
Cover design copyright © 1978 by Joseph del Gaudio
Cover photo copyright © 1978 by Jon Naar

Printed in the United States of America

BONIM BOOKS
a division of Hebrew Publishing Company
80 Fifth Avenue
New York, N.Y. 10011

CONTENTS

foreword   7

light the menorah   11
menorot / candles

spin the dreidel   27
how to play / make your own

decorate a room   31
hangings / wall decorations / table decorations

set a table   41
tablecloths / place mats / napkin holder / napkin rings / trays

have a party   51
invitations / place cards / favors / candy holders

play a game   61
active games / quiet games

put on a show   71
costumes / movies / puppets / theaters

make a gift for the jewish home   79
mezuzot / kippot / wine decanters / mizrahim

make a gift for a . . .   93
book lover / cook / nature lover / traveler / jewelry lover / athlete / grandparent

wrap a gift   121
wrapping paper / gift boxes / package decorations

send a card   **131**
simple cards / relief printing / block printing

index   **140**

about the book/about the author   **143**

key to cover photo   **144**

Foreword

Hanukkah arrives in midwinter. The gloomy cold weather makes us look forward to the gaiety and warmth that surround the Festival of Lights.

One of the lights kindled by this holiday is that of memory. The pages of the calendar flip backward and, once again, I am a young girl in Brooklyn.

The freshly scrubbed kitchen floor is covered with newspapers to keep it clean until the start of the holiday. My brother and I wait impatiently for our grandmother, "Bubba," to start grating potatoes for the traditional latkes (potato pancakes). How eager we are to help make the applesauce—one of the few dishes that we liked to sneak a taste of while it was being prepared.

Each night, for the eight nights of Hanukkah, we lit candles as soon as we saw stars in the sky. Our mood was festive as the room began to glow with the gentle, flickering lights of the menorah, the candelabrum. Our father led us in chanting the blessings and singing *Maoz Tzur,* "Rock of Ages." Then we played games with the dreidel, a four-sided spinning top.

Gift-giving is a Hanukkah custom. In our home, the children received Hanukkah *gelt* (money; for us, it was always coins) and foil-covered chocolate coins. We gave our Jewish teachers in public school, as well as our Hebrew school teachers, small, practical presents.

During our holiday get-togethers, Bubba reminisced about Hanukkah celebrations when she was a child in Russia. From her, I learned the story of the holiday:

About 2,100 years ago, Jewish people worshipped God in the Temple in Jerusalem. The land was ruled by the Syrian king, Antiochus IV. He wanted all the people to follow the Greek religion. He wrecked much of the beautiful Temple, set up pagan idols in it, and enslaved many Jews.

An elderly priest named Mattathias, with his five sons, inspired our people to remain loyal to God. They organized a small army of untrained, but brave, men. One of the sons, Judah Maccabee (his name means "the hammer"), became the leader.

The courage of the Jews—fighting for their religion and homeland—made them victorious over the large, powerful Syrian army. The people threw the idols out of the Temple, cleaned it, and made it ready for worship again. When they were ready to rededicate the Temple, they found enough pure oil to light the menorah for just one day. Miraculously, it remained burning for eight days, until they could prepare more oil.

From that time on, we celebrate Hanukkah, the festival of Lights and Dedication, for eight days, starting on the 25th of the Hebrew month of Kislev.

Time passes and now it is my own four children who are "secretly" taking tastes from the applesauce bowl. We add new family traditions by creating our own customs. Although Hanukkah is considered one of the minor holidays of the Jewish year, we enjoy the extensive preparations for a multifaceted celebration.

Our home is strewn with handcrafted objects. We have expanded our family tradition of giving *gelt* to include token gifts. We make decorative items, things for ceremonial use all year round, or just for fun. A gift may consist of a "promise paper," a list of activities to be shared with one child at a time. Hanging paper dreidels that dance at the slightest breeze, dipping candles, printing greeting cards, and giving parties add a contagious note of festivity to the household.

I teach a creative crafts program in a synagogue Hebrew school. My students don't just talk about Hanukkah as being a happy holiday; they work to enrich their celebration of it. The children's influence reaches into their parents' homes. One father said to me, "Now my child not only wants us to light the menorah at home, she wants to craft one, too."

J.B.
Edison, New Jersey
February 1978
I Adar 5738

HANUKKAH CRAFTS

Light the Menorah

The menorah (plural, *menorot*) is a special lamp or candelabrum used during the holiday of Hanukkah. The menorah holds eight candles plus a helper candle called the *shamash*.

It is possible to make many designs of the menorah, but traditionally the candleholders are arranged in a straight line on the same level. The *shamash* may be placed anywhere, as long as it is clearly apart from the other candles.

Traditional *menorot* had wicks and burned oil. Today, most *menorot* are made to hold small, thin candles. This section provides instructions for making hand-rolled and hand-dipped candles.

On the first night, use the *shamash* to light one candle (or one wick) on the right side of the menorah. On the second night, two candles are placed on the right side and lit from left to right. On the third night, three candles are lit, and so on for eight nights.

The total number of candles used for all eight nights of Hanukkah is 44:

1 plus the *shamash* the first night
2 plus the *shamash* the second night
3 plus the *shamash* the third night
4 plus the *shamash* the fourth night
5 plus the *shamash* the fifth night
6 plus the *shamash* the sixth night
7 plus the *shamash* the seventh night
8 plus the *shamash* the eighth night

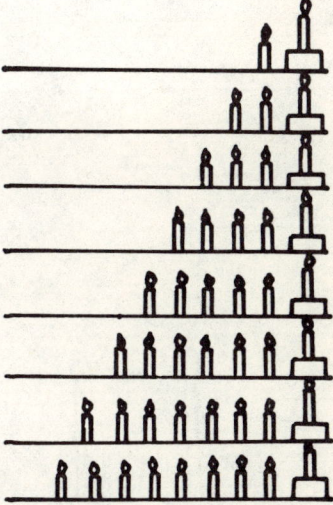

Simple Menorot

PAPER CUP MENORAH

Start with ten small paper nut cups. Fill eight with sand.

To make the holder for the *shamash*, glue the bottom of one cup to the bottom of another cup. Fill the top one with sand. To use, place the cups in a row and insert a Hanukkah candle into the sand in each one.

FLOWER POT MENORAH

Start with eight small clay flower pots (the size used for tiny cacti) and one larger clay pot for the *shamash*. Turn them upside down.

Paint a design on each pot with acrylics. Let dry. Wiggle a candle into the drain hole in each pot. If the candle is too small for the hole, fill in with candle or floral adhesive (from craft store).

You may store the flower pot menorah from year to year by stacking the pots.

Clay Menorot

Many types of modeling materials are available in craft stores:

clay that remains soft	clay that "fires" hard in home oven
clay that air hardens	clay that must be fired in a kiln

You may add decorative marks with any pointed tool—toothpick, knife, or the tines of a fork. Before any of the menorot dry, mark off nine evenly spaced holes. Insert a candle and wiggle slightly to enlarge each hole. To use, you may place a clay menorah on a base of varnished wood, a metal tray, or heavy-duty cardboard covered with household aluminum foil.

COIL METHOD

Coil clay around each candle, one at a time. To raise the *shamash*, make one coil slightly higher. Pinch the ends of the coils together to make one long row.

SLAB METHOD

With a rolling pin, roll out a thick slab of clay. To raise the *shamash*, add a dab of clay.

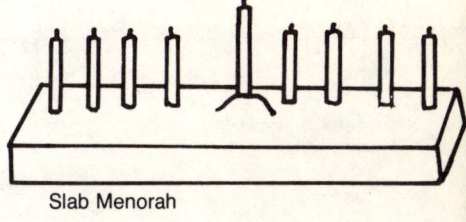
Slab Menorah

PINCH-POT METHOD

Roll ten balls of clay. For a decorative effect, lightly pinch each ball between your thumb and forefinger. Place nine balls in a row. To raise the *shamash*, press the tenth ball on top of one of the others. Flatten the bottom of the balls so they stand securely on the base.

BRAIDED METHOD

Divide a lump of clay into three chunks. Roll each chunk into a rope and braid the ropes together. You may use a different color of clay for each coil in the braid. Flatten the bottom so it stands securely. Build up the clay that will hold the *shamash* candle.

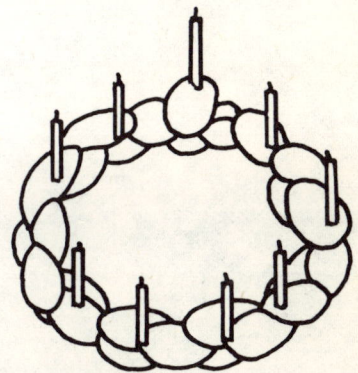
Braided Menorah

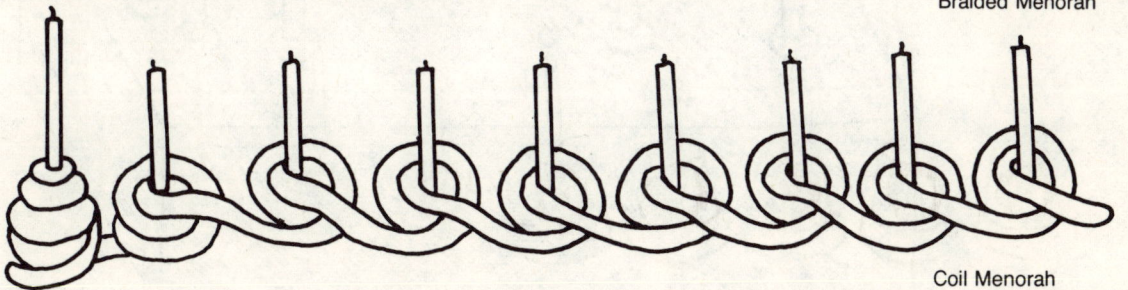
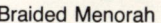
Coil Menorah

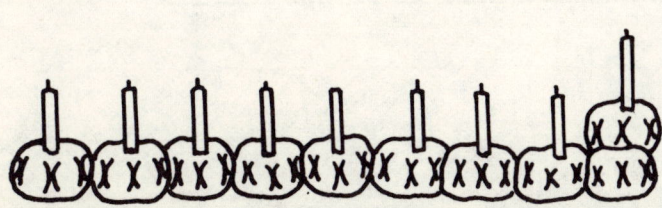
Pinch Pot Menorah

Thimble Menorah

Materials:

styrofoam block (from a packing crate or craft store)
heavy-duty household aluminum foil
scissors or awl
9 thimbles
Hanukkah candles

Optional: candle or floral adhesive (craft store)

Method:
1. Cover the styrofoam block with foil. The foil makes the menorah safe for use.
2. Using the scissors or awl, punch nine evenly spaced holes through the foil and deep into the styrofoam; wiggle the cutting tool to enlarge each hole.
3. To make eight candleholders, push a thimble into each hole until only the rim shows.
4. To raise the *shamash* slightly higher, push the ninth thimble only partially into the foam, just enough to make it secure.
5. To make the candles stand securely in the thimbles, soften the wax by holding the bottom of each candle over a flame. You may use candle or floral adhesive instead. Insert the candles in the thimbles.

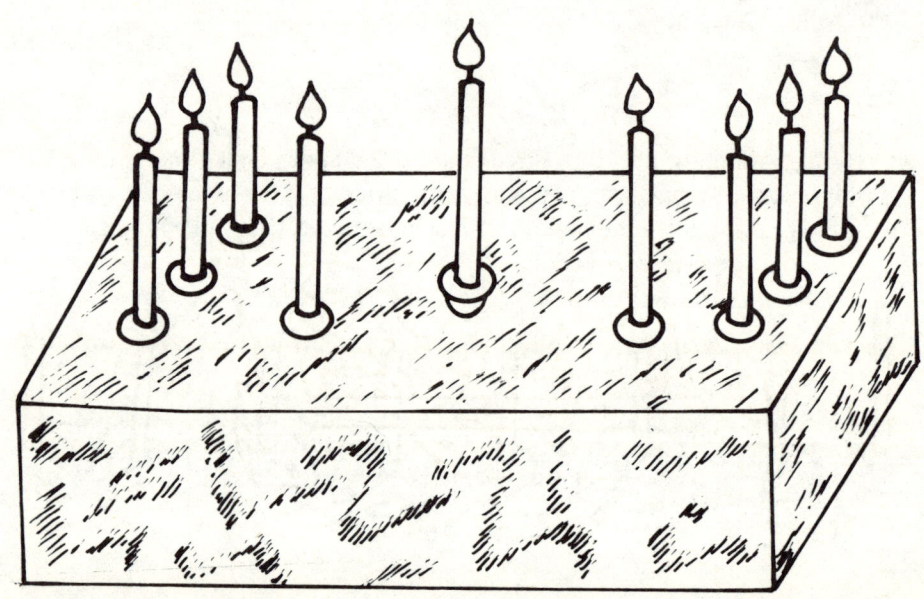

Spackle Menorah

Materials:

1 egg carton, styrofoam or cardboard
scissors
styrofoam (from merchandise packing in cartons, available from gift, appliance, or variety store)
spackle (hardware store)
putty knife or palette knife
Hanukkah candles

Method:

1. Cut apart nine cups from an egg carton. Cut off the points from the top of eight egg cups, making rounded tops. Cut into the sides of the remaining cup to form additional points.
2. Using the knife, cover the top and sides of the styrofoam base with spackle. Then spackle the outside and inside of each cup.
3. Cement each cup to the styrofoam base with spackle. To make the *shamash*, use extra spackle under the painted cup to raise it.
4. Place a dab of spackle in the bottom of each cup. Insert a candle in each dab and wiggle it to make the holes slightly larger. The indentation should be deep enough to hold the candle when the spackle dries.
5. Let the spackle set completely before inserting the candles. The spackle gives the finished menorah an interesting texture and handcrafted look.

Gumdrop Candy Menorah

Materials:

wood base, 3½" × 12"
sandpaper
rag
varnish stain (from hardware, paint, or home supply store)
10 gumdrop candies with a center hole (supermarket or variety store)
wood glue or white glue that dries clear
heavy-duty household aluminum foil
Hanukkah candles

Method:
1. Following the grain of the wood, sand the base until smooth. Wipe the sanding off the wood.
2. With a rag, stain and varnish the wood base, using this one-step product.
3. Decide where you want to place the gumdrops on the wood. To make the *shamash*, glue two candies together. Apply a coat of glue to the bottom of each candy, including the candies for the *shamash*, and place on the wood. Let dry.
4. Place the bottom of a candle on the center of a little square of foil. Gather the foil around the candle base. Insert the foil-bottomed candle into the hole in the candy. Repeat for the remaining eight candles.

    The varnish on the wood and the foil collar around the bottom of the candle make the menorah safe for use.

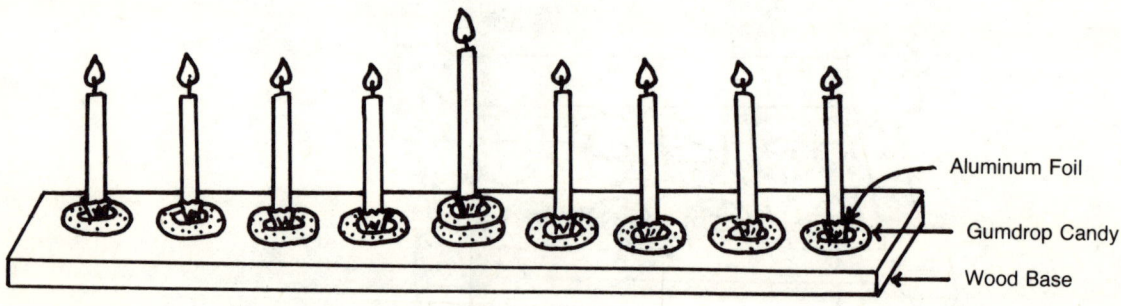

Candleholder Menorah

Materials:

wood base, about 6″ × 9″ (from craft store)
wood block, about 2″ square (craft store)
varnish stain (hardware, paint, or home supply store)
8 metal candleholders (craft store)
white glue
Hanukkah candles

Optional: drill, candle, or floral adhesive (craft store)

Method:

1. Stain and varnish the wood base and the wood block with this one-step product. Let dry. The varnish makes the menorah safe for use.
2. Screw eight candleholders in a pleasing arrangement into the wood base. If the base is made of hard wood, drill holes before screwing in the candleholders.
3. To make the *shamash*, glue the block of wood to the base. Let dry. Screw the ninth candleholder into the block.
4. To make the candles stand securely in their holders, soften the wax at the bottom of each candle by holding it over a flame. You may use candle or floral adhesive instead. Insert the candles in the holders.

Plaster Cast Menorah

Materials:

1 empty milk carton
scissors
1 styrofoam egg carton
water
salad oil
paper towels
newspapers
powdered craft plaster (from craft store)
stick
fine sandpaper
craft cement
Hanukkah candles

Optional: watercolor paints, brush, varnish (spray or brush on)

Method:

1. Open the top seam on the milk carton so it becomes a disposable bucket. Wash it, then dry thoroughly.
2. Cut the lid off the egg carton. Pour water into the lid and into each egg cup. Empty the water into the milk carton.
3. Using a paper towel, rub the inside of the lid and the inside of each cup with salad oil.
4. Cover the work surface with newspapers. Gradually add the powdered plaster to the water in the milk carton, until the water will not absorb any more plaster. Stir the mixture with the stick until it is smooth.
5. Pour the mixture into the oiled lid and cups. Tap the bottom of the filled containers on a hard surface to remove any air bubbles. Do not pour leftover plaster down the drain. Clean your hands with paper towels.
6. When the plaster is partially set (allow about 15 minutes), insert a candle in the center of each plaster-filled cup. Wiggle it slightly to

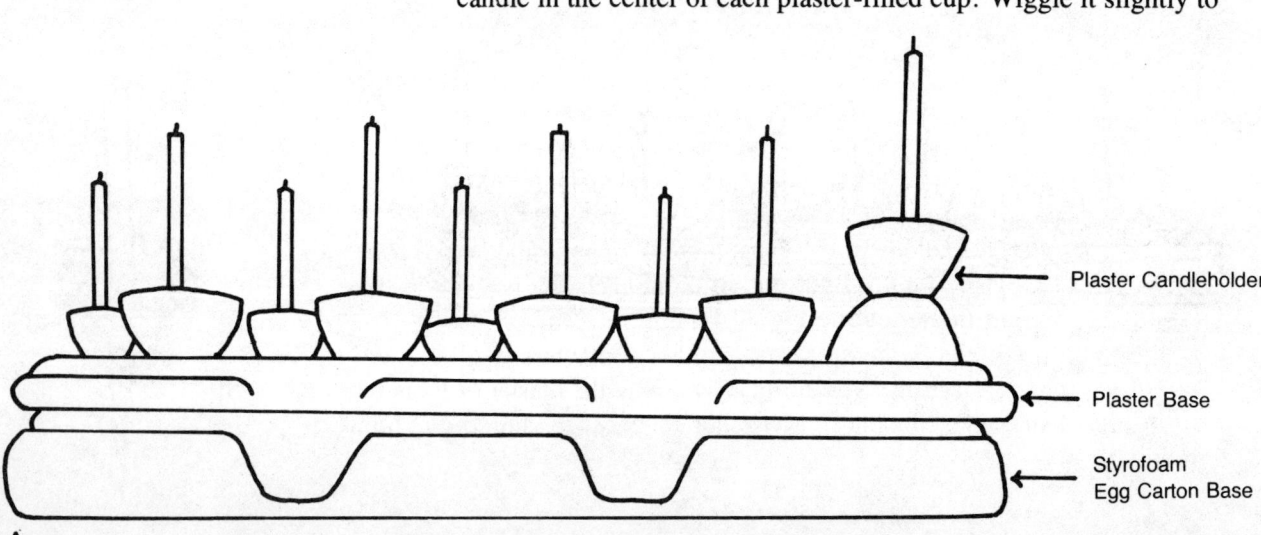

enlarge the candle hole. Remove the candle and let plaster set completely for one-half hour or more. Powdered craft plaster dries more slowly than plaster of Paris. It has a smoother look and is also less brittle.
7. When the plaster is dry, push the underside of the containers and the molded plaster pieces will pop out.
8. Lightly sand any areas you want smoother.
9. Place the lid of the egg carton on a table, top up. Cement the mold from the lid on top of this (figure A).
10. To make the *shamash,* cement the narrow ends of two candleholders together (figure B).
11. Cement all the molded candleholders to the lid mold (figure A). Let dry.
12. Paint the completed menorah with watercolors and protect with a coat of varnish if you wish.

Egg-shaped Menorah

Materials:

9 raw eggs	plaster of Paris
small, sharp scissors (manicure)	disposable container
bowl	stick
cooking oil	paper towels
9 egg cups or other small containers	small knife
	Hanukkah candles
newspapers	

Optional: tempera, acrylic, or oil paint, brush

Method:
1. Gently shake each egg to loosen the contents. Cut a hole ¾" across in the larger end of each shell. Empty the contents into a bowl. Refrigerate and save for cooking.
2. Pour a little oil into one of the eggs, swirl it around, and pour it into the next egg. Continue until the inside of each egg is coated with oil. Discard the leftover oil.
3. Prop up the shells in the egg cups or other containers.
4. Cover the work surface with newspapers. Mix the plaster of Paris in the disposable container, according to package directions. Stir

with the stick. The completed mixture should look like heavy cream.
5. Slowly pour the plaster into each shell until it is filled. Do not pour leftover plaster down the drain. Clean your hands with paper towels.
6. After the plaster has completely dried (allow several hours), carefully crack the shells and peel off.
7. With the knife, carve a hole in the small end of each egg, big enough to hold a candle.
8. For a different look, you may pour the plaster into unoiled, empty shells. Let it harden. Leave the shell on the "egg." With the knife, carve the candle hole through the shell and into the plaster.
9. To raise the *shamash,* place one candleholder in a small, colorful egg cup.
10. Paint the completed menorah, if you wish.
11. To use, place the candleholders in a row and insert a Hanukkah candle in each one.

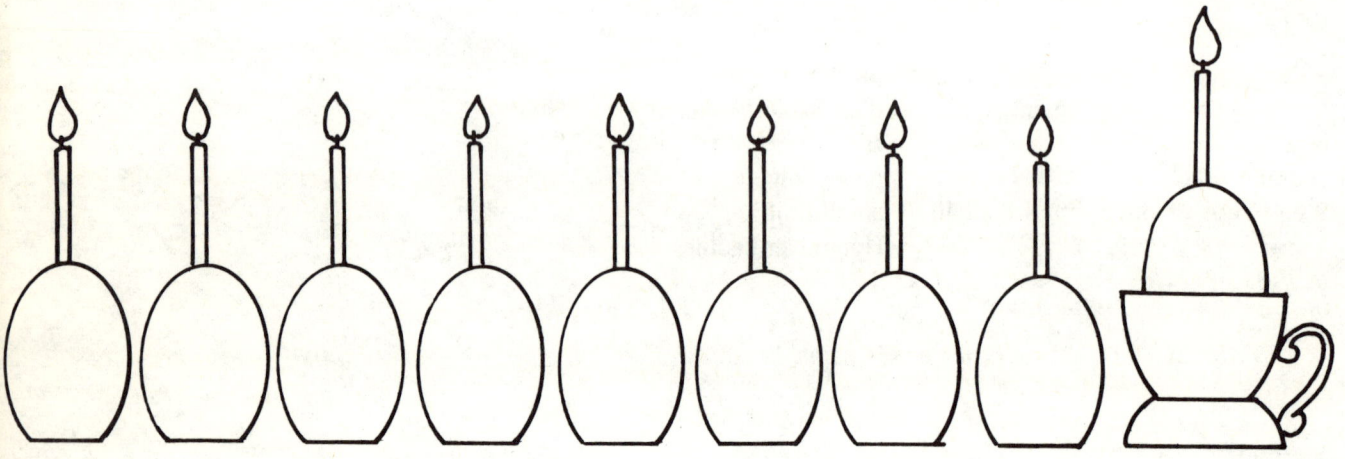

Oil Menorah

Materials:

8 small, heavy-duty glasses
1 large, heavy-duty glass
water
salad oil
scissors
sheet cork, thin enough to float (from craft store)
wax paper
pointed tool (skewer, awl)
27" wick with wire core (craft store)

Optional: glass stain, food coloring, colored stones

Method:

1. You may decorate the outside of the glasses with glass stain, add food coloring to the water, or place colored stones at the bottoms of the glasses.
2. Fill all the glasses until three-fourths full with water and oil. The mixture in each glass should be two-thirds water and one-third oil. The oil will rise to the top.
3. Cut a small square of cork. Cover the top with a square of wax paper the same size. With the pointed tool, puncture a hole through the center of both.
4. Cut the wick into 54 pieces, each ½" long. A total of 44 wicks are needed for all eight nights of Hanukkah. You may save the remaining wicks for next Hanukkah, along with the reusable cork and wax paper.
5. To make one candle, thread one length of wick through both cork and wax paper. The longer part of the wick should stick out of the wax paper side (figure A).
6. To prevent the cork from burning, coat the wax paper with oil. Place the wick, cork side down, on top of the oil in the glass (figure B). Light the wicks. The wicks will burn for many hours, depending upon the amount of oil used.

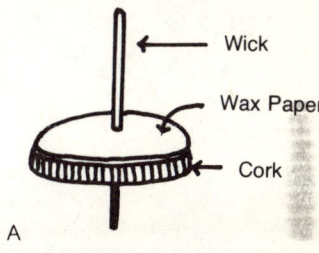

A

B

Clothespin Menorah

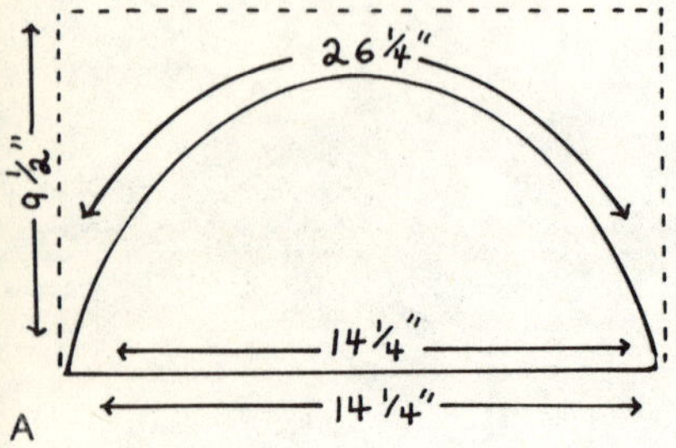

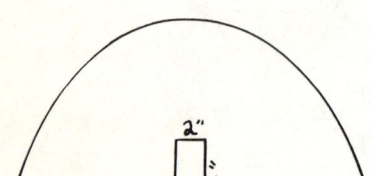

Materials:

1 piece of wood, 14¼" long × 9½" wide
saw
sandpaper
1 piece of wood, 4" long × 2" wide
white glue
spray or brush-on paint, any color, or wood stain
9 clip clothespins
9 screws (see step 4)
screwdriver
varnish, spray or brush-on
Hanukkah candles

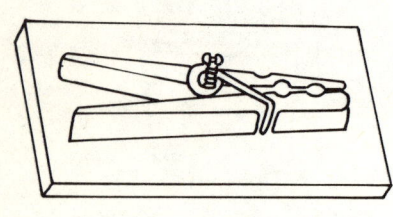

Method:

1. Saw the large piece of wood into a half-circle, as shown in figure A. Sand any rough areas.
2. Glue the smaller piece of wood to the wood half-circle (figure B). Let dry.
3. Paint or stain the wood base and the clothespins. Let dry.
4. The screws should be narrow enough to fit in the hole in the metal spiral of the clothespin with the head of the screw resting on top. They should be long enough to go through the clothespin and grip into the wood base. With the screwdriver, screw one clothespin to the small piece of wood (figure C).
5. Arrange the rest of the clothespins on the large piece of wood (figure D). Screw each one in place.
6. Protect the menorah with varnish, following the manufacturer's directions. Let dry.
7. To insert a candle, pinch the back of a clothespin to open it and place a candle in the front groove. Release the pressure on the back of the clothespin, which will hold the candle securely.

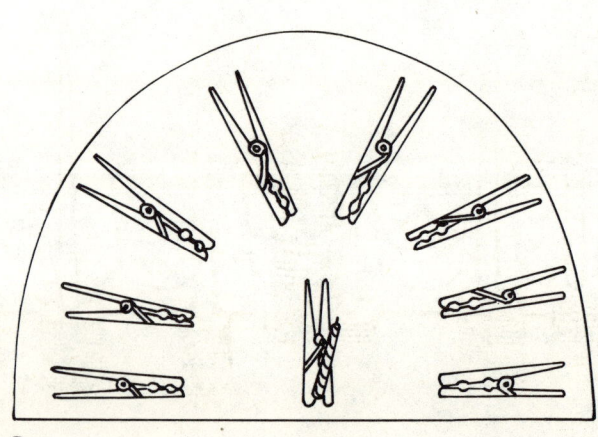

Spool Menorah

Materials:

1 piece of wood, 12" long × 4" wide × ½" thick
wood varnish stain (from hardware, paint, or home supply store)
brush
4 small beads (craft store)
white glue
heavy-duty household aluminum foil
pencil
10 spools of thread, assorted colors
Hanukkah candles

Optional: knife

Method:

1. To make the menorah base, stain the piece of wood. Let dry.
2. To make the little feet, glue a bead to each corner of the bottom of the wood. Let dry.
3. To make the candleholders, place a spool on foil, trace around it, and cut out. Cut out nine foil circles. Glue a circle of foil to one end of each spool. Arrange eight spools, foil side up, on the base. Glue in place and let dry.
4. To make the *shamash,* glue two spools together and glue to base.
5. Poke a hole through the foil on each spool, to coincide with the hole in the spool.
6. Place the bottom of a candle on the center of a little square of foil. Gather the foil around the candle base. Insert the foil-bottomed candle into the hole in the spool. If the candle is too wide for the hole, use a knife to shave away some wax.

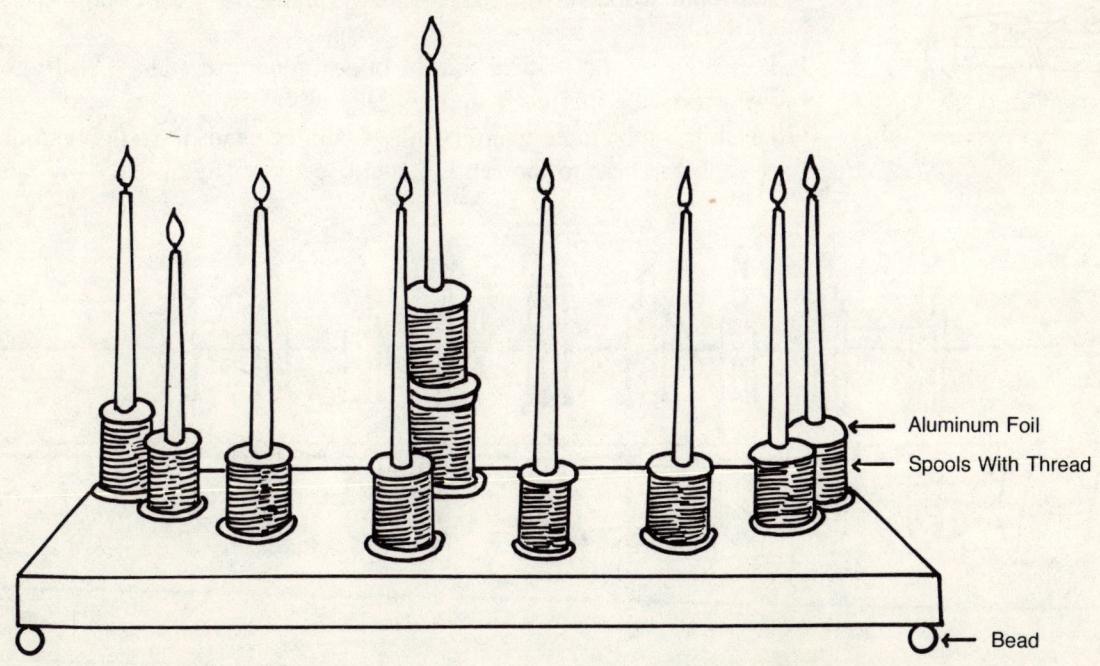

Test Tube Menorah

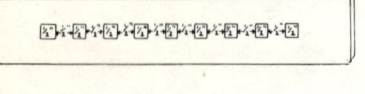

A

B

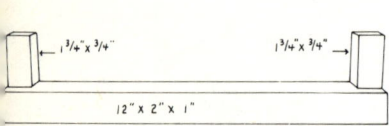

C

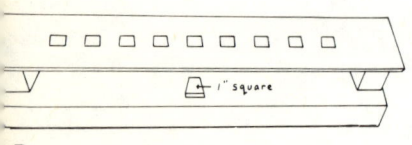

D

Materials:

basswood:
   1 piece 22″ long × 3″ wide × ⅛″ thick
   1 piece 12″ long × 2″ wide × 1″ thick
   2 pieces, each about 1¾″ long × ¾″ wide
   1 piece 1″ square × ½″ thick
pencil
ruler
craft knife
9 glass test tubes, each 4″ long (from hobby store)
fine sandpaper
white glue
varnish stain (craft, paint, or hardware store)
brush
colored sand (craft store)
Hanukkah candles

Optional: toy blocks or empty spools of thread

Method:

1. Draw nine squares, each ½″, on the large piece of wood. Center them on the wood, ½″ apart, as shown in figure A.
2. With the craft knife, carefully cut out each ½″ square (figure B). A test tube should be able to fit securely into each opening. Lightly sand the wood.
3. To make the base of the menorah, place the two small pieces of wood on top of either side of the medium piece of wood. You may use toy blocks or empty spools of thread instead of the 2 small pieces of wood (figure C).
4. Glue the large piece of wood with the square cutouts to the top of the small pieces of wood (figure D). To raise the *shamash,* glue the 1″ square of wood on the base, directly under the middle hole (figure D).
5. Protect the menorah with a coat of one-step varnish stain. Let dry.
6. Insert a test tube into each square hole.
7. Fill each test tube three quarters full of colored sand. Push the bottom of each candle into the sand to stand securely (figure E).

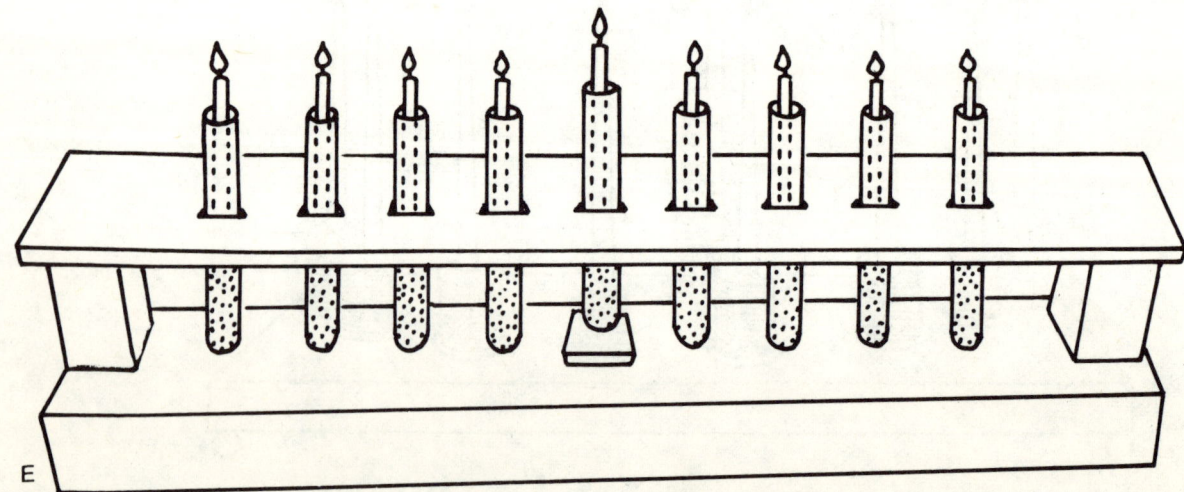

E

Hand-rolled Hanukkah Candles

Materials:

1 sheet of honeycomb beeswax, about 8" × 16½", any color (from craft store)

scissors
wick (craft store)

Method:

1. To make one candle, cut approximately a 2½" strip from the sheet of wax (figure A).
2. Cut the 2½" strip in half (figure B).
3. Place the wick along one of the edges of the cut strip (figure C).
4. Roll the wax strip tightly around the wick. Cut the wick even with the bottom of the candle. If necessary, trim the top of the wick to about ¼" in length (figure D).
5. Repeat steps 1–4 to make more candles.

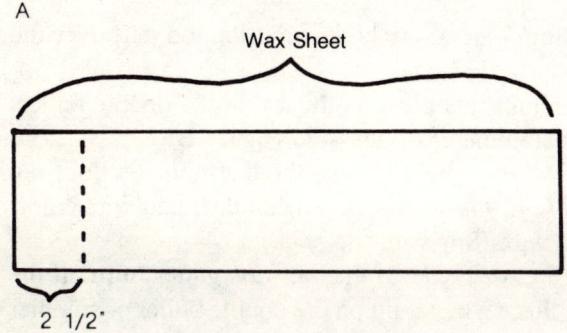
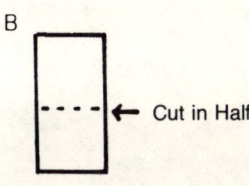
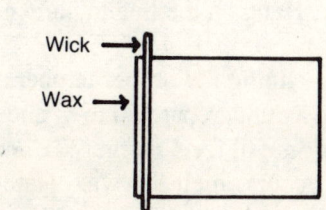
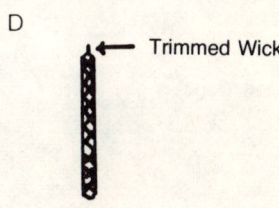

Hand-dipped Hanukkah Candles

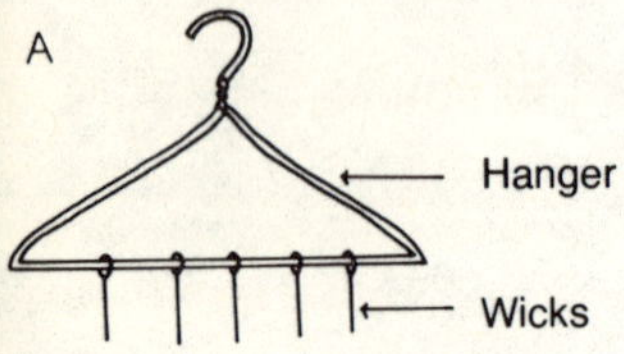

Materials:

wick with wire core (from craft store)
scissors
wood or wire clothes hangers
water
wax (craft store)
double boiler (see step 11)
candy thermometer
stick
cord
newspapers

Optional: orange wax coloring, oil paint, or poster paint, metal pot lid or baking soda

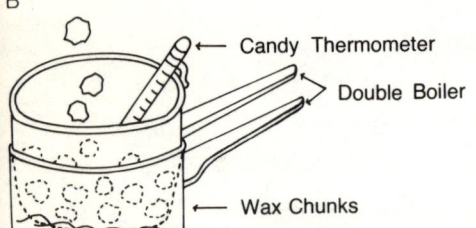

Method:

1. Cut the wick into 5" lengths.
2. Tie one end of a wick around the bottom bar of a hanger (figure A). Add as many wicks, spaced about 1" apart, as will fit into the top of the double boiler without touching the sides. Repeat with the other hangers.
3. Add water to the bottom part of the boiler. Put the top part over the bottom part.
4. Break the wax into chunks and place in the top of the double boiler. Hook the candy thermometer on the side (figure B).
5. Melt the wax over low heat, checking that the thermometer does not exceed 200 degrees. If you want colored candles, add wax coloring or paint to the wax. Stir with the stick.
6. Note: Use EXTREME CAUTION. If the hot wax ignites, turn off the heat immediately. Place a metal lid on the double boiler or smother the flame with baking soda.
7. String cord across the room to make a line to hold the hangers while the wax cools and hardens. Place newspapers on the floor under the cord to catch wax drippings.
8. Dip the wicks into the melted wax. Hang on the line to harden (figure C). Repeat with the next hanger.
9. The trick to candle dipping is maintaining the proper temperature for the melted wax. If too hot, the wax undercoat will melt and no new wax will adhere. If too cold, a skin will form on the wax and it will not give a proper coat. If this occurs, melt the wax again.
10. Continue dipping until the candles are as thick as you like.
11. Note: a thin layer of wax will remain in the double boiler. Use the double boiler only for crafts projects, not for food.
12. Remove the cooled candles from the hangers and trim the wicks to about a ¼" length.

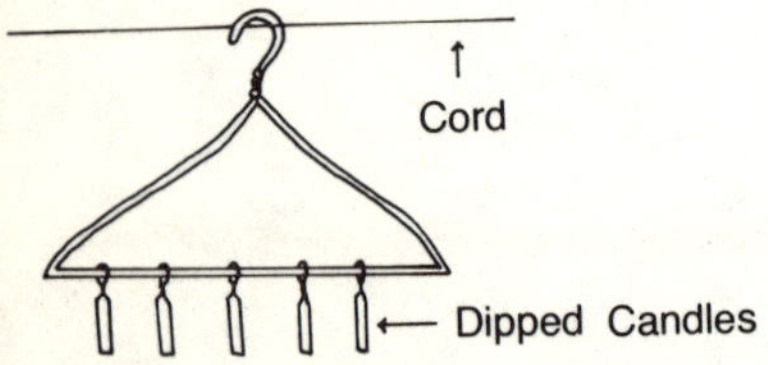

Spin the Dreidel

A dreidel (Hebrew, *sevivon*) is a spinning top, with a Hebrew letter on each of its four sides. The letters stand for *nes gadol ha-yah shahm,* "a great miracle happened there"—the miracle of Hanukkah.

You may craft a dreidel from wood, wax, erasers, large beads, or any other material that can be molded into a shape. To make it spin, insert a sharpened pencil, pointed dowel, or long nail.

To play the traditional dreidel game, give each player the same number of nuts or coins. To start, each player puts one nut or coin in the middle of the playing area.

If the dreidel lands on a		It means the player
nun	נ	wins nothing
gimmel	ג	wins everything in the middle
hay	ה	wins half of the middle pile
shin	ש	puts one nut or coin in the middle

After someone spins a *gimmel,* all the players put one nut or coin in the middle. Continue taking turns until time is up or until each player has had a specified number of turns. The player with the most nuts or coins wins.

Egg Carton

Ping Pong Ball

Clay

Simple Dreidels

EGG CARTON DREIDEL

Cut a cup from the bottom of a styrofoam or cardboard egg carton. Cut deeply into the cup to make four pointed petals. Insert a sharpened pencil, pointed dowel, or long nail through the bottom of the cup.

With a ball-point pen, add one of the Hebrew letters below on each of the four sides.

PING PONG BALL DREIDEL

With small scissors (manicure) or a skewer, poke a hole through a ping pong ball. Insert a dowel (from craft store) which has been sharpened to a point. With felt-tip pens, print the Hebrew letters below around the ball. Let dry.

CLAY DREIDEL

Mold a dreidel from clay that "fires" hard in a home oven. Let dry. Bake the clay according to package directions. Let cool.

Leave the clay its natural color or decorate with acrylic paints. Paint one of the Hebrew letters below on each of the four sides. Let dry.

WHEEL WITH A COLLAR DREIDEL

Start with a wood or plastic wheel from a toy car, bead set, or building peg and block set. Glue a square paper or cardboard "collar" around the wheel.

Paint the Hebrew letters below around the wheel. Let dry. Insert a sharpened dowel through the hole in the wheel.

TOOTHPICK AND BUTTON DREIDEL

Start with a white button that has two holes. With a felt-tip pen, print the Hebrew letters below around the button. Push a round toothpick through each hole and glue or tape the bottoms together.

To spin the dreidel, squeeze the tops of the toothpicks together. The heavier the button, the faster and longer the spin.

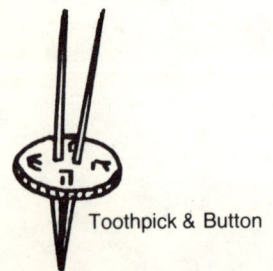

Wheel With a Collar

Toothpick & Button

Stapled Cardboard Dreidel

Materials:

light cardboard or poster board
scissors
pencil or pointed dowel
stapler
crayons

Method:

1. Cut two dreidel shapes out of light cardboard or poster board.
2. Place the pencil or dowel between the two shapes. Staple the sides together, keeping as close to the dowel as possible (figure A).
3. To form four "sides," fold back the protruding flaps. With crayons, draw one of the Hebrew letters below on each of the four sides (figure B).

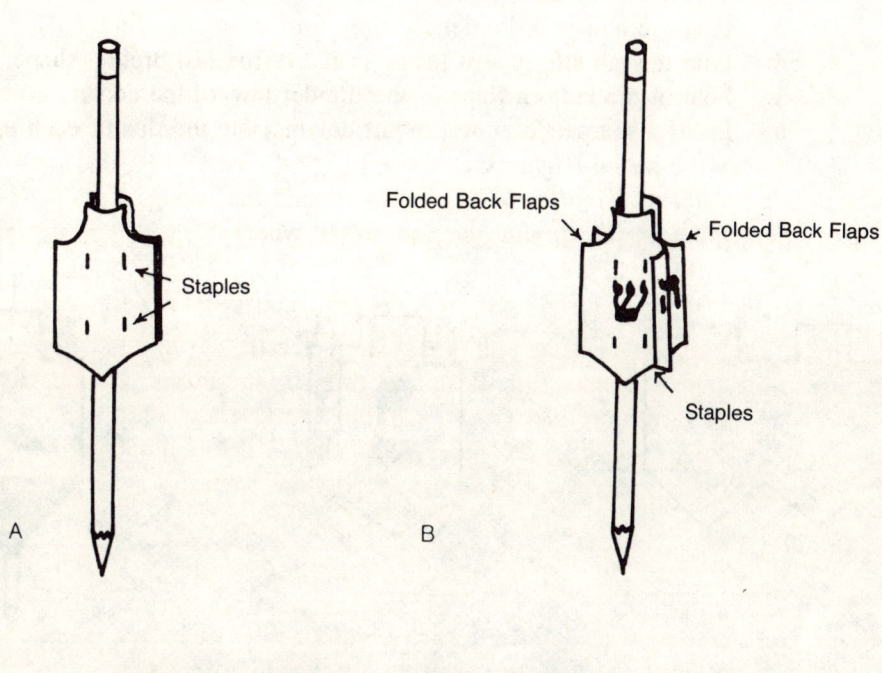

Poster Board Dreidel

Materials:

poster board or heavy construction
    paper
pencil
scissors
acrylic paints, any color
brush
glue
sharpened pencil

Method:

1. On a piece of poster board or heavy construction paper, draw four attached dreidels and a tab, as shown in figure A. Cut out the drawing.
2. With acrylic paints, add one of the Hebrew letters below on each of the four sides. Let dry.
3. Fold the attached dreidels so they form a square (figure B).
4. Fold the tab and glue it to the inside of the last dreidel shape.
5. Fold in the bottom flaps of the dreidel toward the center.
6. Insert a sharpened pencil, point down. Glue the tips of each point to the pencil (figure C).

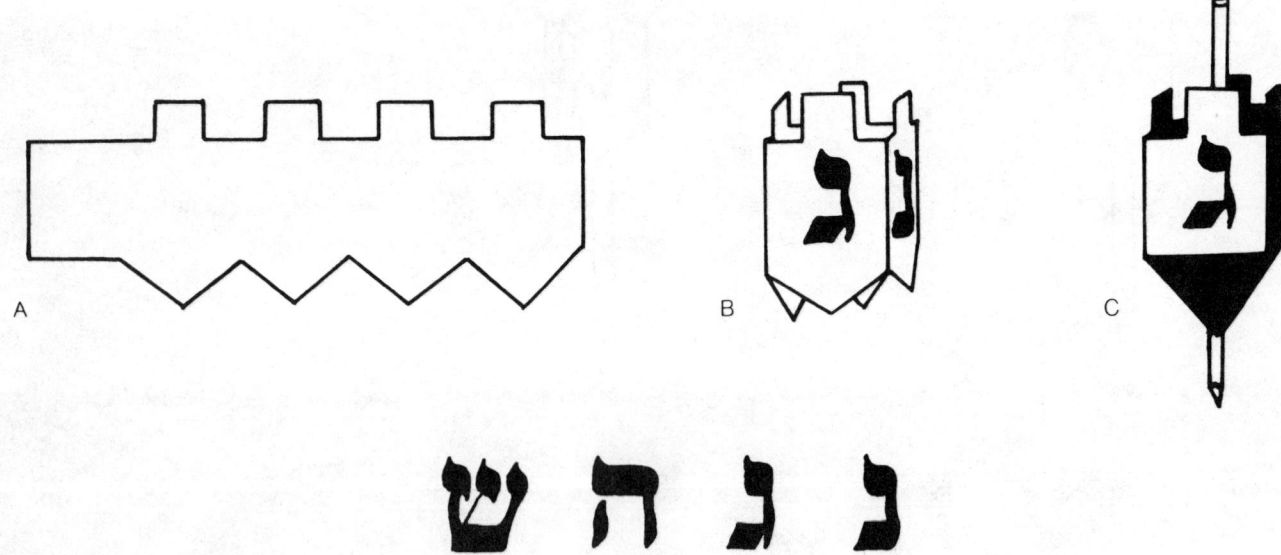

Decorate a Room

Add to the holiday festivity by making decorations to hang around the room, suspend from the ceiling, or place on the table as a centerpiece. Make a cartoon mural for color, a pomander dreidel for fragrance, and a swinging chain of paper stars for movement. These decorations add drama and fun to the home or classroom.

Simple Decorations

CARTOON MURAL

Tape together several sheets of construction paper to form one long sheet. Place the sheet, tape side down, on the work surface. With felt-tip pens, crayons, or poster paint, draw Hanukkah symbols scattered all over the sheet. Turn each symbol into a cartoon by adding facial features, arms, and legs. Tape the mural to a wall.

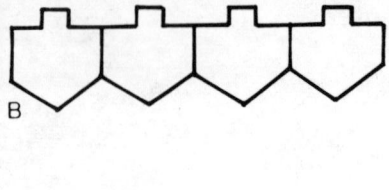

PAPER SYMBOL CHAIN

Cut Hanukkah symbols from colored construction paper. Cut plastic drinking straws into thirds.

With a wide-eyed needle, punch two holes, about one-half inch apart, near the top of each cutout. Thread the needle with yarn or cord.

Weave the yarn through each hole, separating each cutout symbol from the next with a section of the straw. To hang, tape each end of the yarn from one wall to another or across the ceiling.

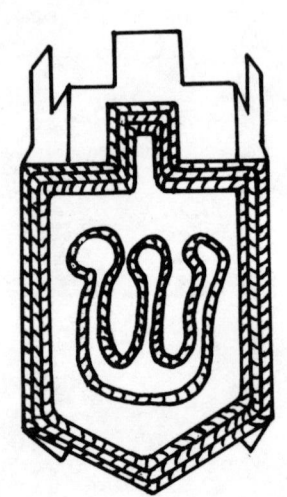

STANDING DREIDEL

Start with a large rectangular sheet of sturdy paper or thin cardboard (or tape several sheets of paper together). Fold the paper into four even sections.

On the top section, draw a dreidel with one part of the design touching each side of the paper (figure A). Cut out the dreidel, taking care not to cut through the fold. Unfold (figure B). Decorate with colored pencils, crayons, or poster paint, or glue on pieces of colored paper, fabric, or yarn.

To make the dreidel stand, fold it, decorated side out, so that each dreidel becomes one side of a square (figure C). Tape the open edges together on the inside. Stand on a table or shelf.

Standing Dreidel

Cartoon Mural

Paper Symbol Chain

Macaroni Star

Materials:

lightweight cardboard
pencil
scissors
hole punch
uncooked macaroni, any interesting shape
white glue
wax paper
spray paint, any color
yarn, any color

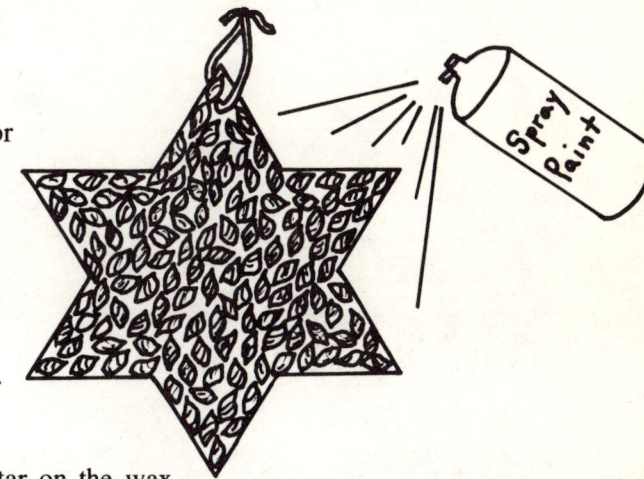

Method:

1. Draw a Star of David on the cardboard and cut it out.
2. Punch a hole in the top of one point of the star.
3. Glue the macaroni to the cardboard. Let dry.
4. Cover the work surface with wax paper. Place the star on the wax paper. Spray paint, making sure all the crevices of the macaroni are painted. Let dry.
5. To hang, thread yarn through the hole and tie the ends.

Corrugated Cardboard Symbol

Materials:

corrugated cardboard from cut apart cartons (from appliance, variety, or food store)
pencil
craft knife
masking tape, any color
glue-on picture hanger

Optional: yarn or colored gravel (craft store or pet shop), white glue

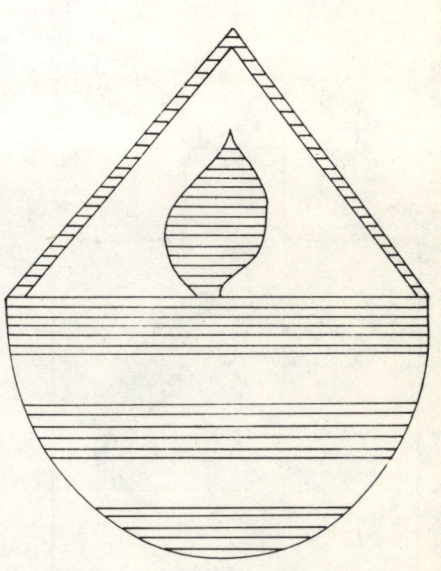

Method:

1. Draw a Hanukkah symbol on the cardboard.
2. Shade the areas of the design you want to cut.
3. With the craft knife, cut away a few layers of the shaded portions of the design, so the ridges of the cardboard show.
4. If the top layer of the cardboard is a different color from the exposed

layer, you may want to leave the design as it is.

If the top layer of the cardboard is the same color as the exposed layer, you may want to:

a. Spread one ridge at a time with glue and cover it with gravel. Let dry. Tilt to remove excess gravel.

b. Run a bead of glue along the ridge between two corrugated humps and place a pre-cut length of yarn on it. Continue until all the ridges are covered with yarn.

5. Cover the edges of the cardboard with the colored masking tape.
6. To hang, attach the picture hanger to the back of the symbol.

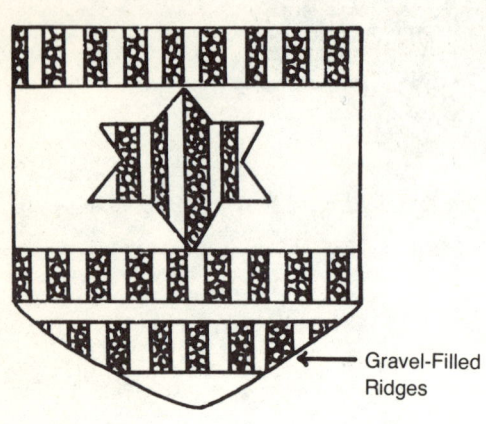
Gravel-Filled Ridges

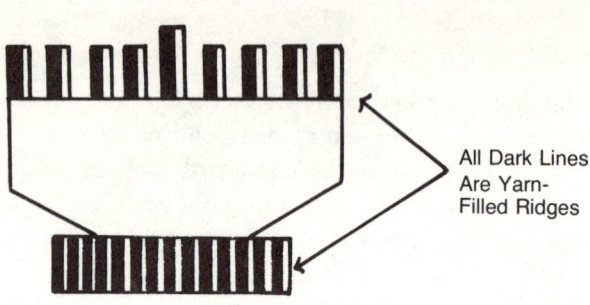
All Dark Lines Are Yarn-Filled Ridges

Mock Pomander Dreidel

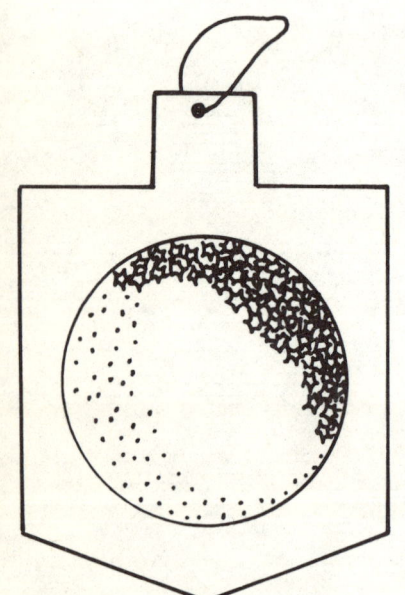

Materials:

small styrofoam ball, to fit the center of the dreidel (from craft store)
serrated knife or craft knife
1 sheet of cardboard
pencil
hole punch

paint, crayons, or felt-tip pens, any colors
whole cloves
ginger
cinnamon
white glue
yarn

Optional: orange or lemon extract

Method:

1. Cut the styrofoam ball in half.
2. Draw a dreidel on the cardboard and cut out.

3. Punch a hole in the top center of the dreidel handle.
4. Decorate one side of the cardboard dreidel.
5. Place one of the halves of the styrofoam ball, flat side down, on the work surface. Push the stem of each clove into the styrofoam until the entire rounded side is covered. For a pleasant scent, you may sprinkle orange or lemon extract on the clove-studded styrofoam.
6. Generously sprinkle ginger and cinnamon over the cloves. Tilt the styrofoam to remove the excess.
7. Glue the flat side of the styrofoam to the center of the decorated side of the dreidel.
8. To hang, tie a loop of yarn through the hole.
9. Repeat steps 2–8 to make another pomander dreidel. Hang several in a room and it will have a pungent aroma.

Corkboard Picture

Materials:

1 piece of cork, thicker than pointed part of tack (from craft store or home supply center)

bulletin board tacks, any colors (stationery store, variety store)
2 sticks or dowels or twigs
craft cement

Optional: yarn, any color, glue-on picture hanger

Method:

1. Arrange the tacks in the cork to form a word or design.
2. You may wind yarn around the tacks to form a border (figure A).
3. To make the cork stand, place cement on the tips of the sticks. Push the cement-coated tips into the back of the cork at an angle (figure B). If you want to hang the picture, attach the glue-on picture hanger to the back.

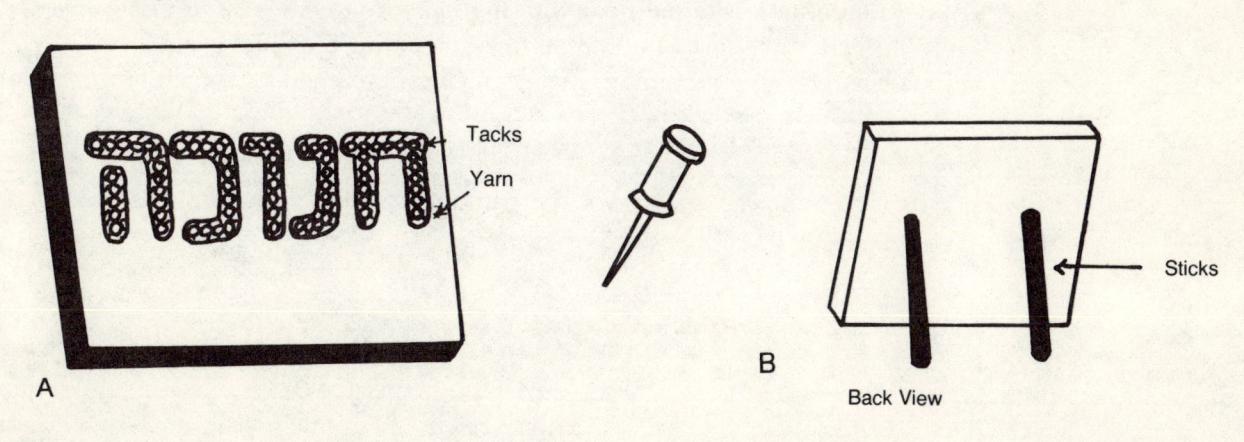

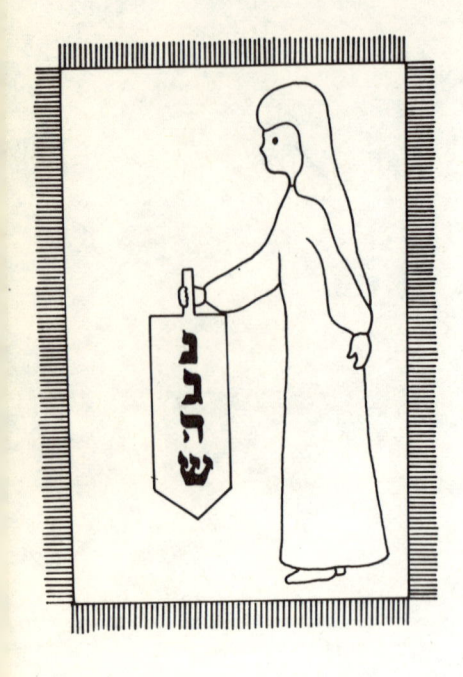

Embroidered Mat

Materials:

heavy fabric (loosely woven wool, coarse linen, or burlap), any size, solid color
paper
pencil
dressmaker's carbon, white if fabric is dark, dark color if fabric is light (from sewing or variety store)
ball-point pen
yarn or embroidery floss, same color as the fabric (the sewing store will help you select the proper yarn for the material)
embroidery needle

Optional: needle and thread (to match the fabric), tubes of liquid embroidery, picture hangers, rug tape (sewing or variety store)

Method:

1. Pull one thread at a time along the edges of the fabric. Unraveling the fabric about 1″ all around makes a pretty fringed border. Always pull the top edge first. If the fabric cannot be fringed, turn the edges under and hem.
2. Sketch a design on the paper.
3. Place the dressmaker's carbon (it doesn't smear) face down on the mat, place the sketch on it, and trace all the lines with a ball-point pen. Carefully lift up one of the corners to be sure all the design has transferred to the fabric. If not, retrace the lines. Remove the pattern and the carbon.
4. Almost any embroidery stitch may be used to outline the design. You may want to fill in some areas of the design with stitches or use liquid embroidery according to package directions.
5. You may hang the mat as a wall decoration. Attach the picture hangers to the back of the mat, near the top.
6. You may use the mat as a rug to sit on. To prevent it from slipping, tack it to the floor with rug tape. You may want to make several small mats for players to sit on during a dreidel game.

Pipe Cleaner Picture

Materials:

styrofoam ball, 1½" in diameter (craft store)
serrated knife or craft knife
pipe cleaners or chenille craft sticks, green and any other colors (from craft or variety store)
1 styrofoam tray
white glue
felt-tip pen, any color
glue-on picture hanger

Method:

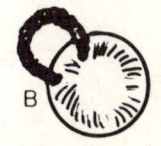

1. Cut the styrofoam ball in half. The flat, cut side of the ball will be the back of the flower.
2. To make the petals, cut several pipe cleaners into 3" lengths. Curve each length (figure A).
3. Insert the curved pipe cleaners along the rim of the ball (figure B).
4. To complete one flower, keep adding rounded pipe cleaner lengths, each overlapping the next (figure C). Make new rows, until the entire rounded surface of this half of the ball is covered (figure D).
5. Twist a full length of green pipe cleaner to form a stem and two leaves. Insert into the ball (figure E).
6. Using the other half of the styrofoam ball, repeat steps 2–5 to make a second flower.
7. To form the letters HANUKKAH, cut eight pipe cleaners into 3" lengths. Shape each one into a letter.
8. Glue the flowers and letters to the styrofoam tray.
9. Using the felt-tip pen, draw a dreidel around each letter.
10. To make grass, glue short pieces of green pipe cleaners to the bottom of the tray (figure F).
11. To hang, attach the glue-on picture hanger.

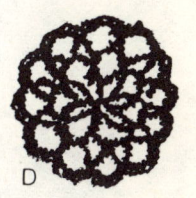

Sand-cast Menorah

Materials:

deep cardboard box top
household aluminum foil
sand (from hardware store or home supply center)
newspapers
water
stick
spoon
plaster of Paris
empty milk carton or other disposable container
paper towels
2 paper clips

Optional: small stones or colored beads

Method:

1. Line the box top with foil. Fill about three-fourths full of sand (figure A).
2. Cover the work surface with newspapers. Carefully pour water onto the sand until it is thoroughly moistened.
3. With the stick and spoon, design one large menorah or several smaller ones in the wet sand. You may want to add a border design.
4. You may add small stones or colored beads for decoration. Press lightly onto the sand (figure B).
5. Pour the plaster of Paris into the disposable container, about three-fourths full. Add water, mixing with your hand or a stick until it is smooth and looks like heavy cream.
6. Carefully and slowly, pour the plaster on the sand design. Do not pour leftover plaster down the drain. Clean your hands with wet paper towels.
7. Before the plaster hardens, place two paper clips, one on each side, on the top back of the plaster cast.
8. When the plaster is dry, lift it out of the sand. Gently brush off the excess sand.

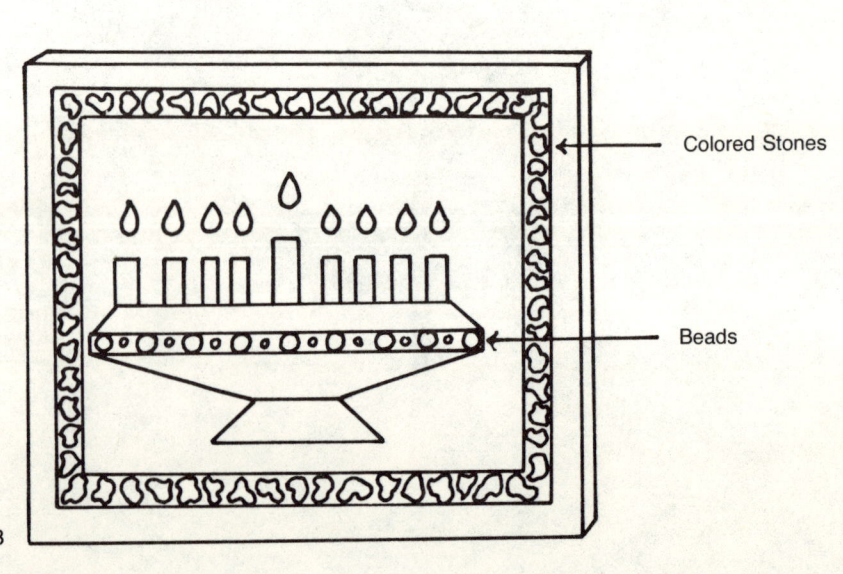

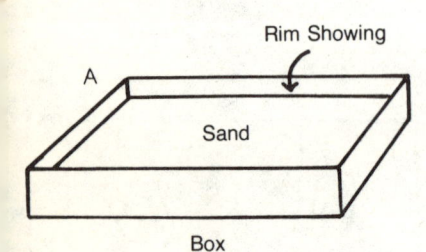

The Five Maccabees on Parade

Materials:

old glove
scissors
cotton batting, tissues, or crumpled paper towels
needle
thread, same color as glove
movable eyes (from craft store) or buttons
scraps of yarn, fabric, trim, and pompoms
white glue
Israeli flag picks (from party goods store or synagogue gift shop, or make your own with paper and toothpicks)
heavy cardboard, wood, or box top

Method:

1. Cut the fingers off the glove, as shown by the dotted lines in figure A.
2. To make one Maccabee, stuff one finger with cotton batting (figure B). Sew the opening closed (figure C).
3. Decorate the Maccabee by gluing on eyes, fabric scraps, and trim.
4. You may tuck a flag into the trim around the figure or stick it into the figure itself.
5. Repeat steps 2–4 to make four more Maccabees.
6. Glue the Maccabees to a cardboard, wood, or box top base.

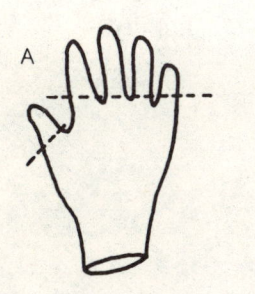

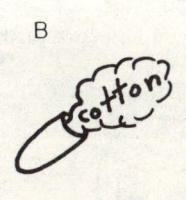

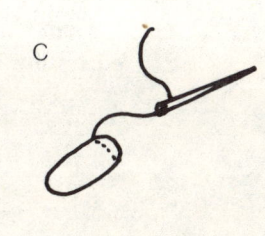

Bottle Doll

Materials:

1 plastic detergent bottle without cover
1 styrofoam ball (craft store)
household aluminum foil
permanent felt-tip pen, black
glass stain, any colors (from craft store)
brush
styrofoam ring (craft store)
construction paper, same size as styrofoam ring
white craft cement
artificial flowers or leaves (craft or variety store)
solvent to clean brush (craft store)

Method:

1. Remove the bottle top. To make the doll's body and head, push the styrofoam ball onto the neck of the bottle.
2. Wrap the bottle and styrofoam ball with foil. Be sure the foil is smooth on the bottom of the bottle so the doll will stand.
3. Outline the features on the face and details on the costume with the felt-tip pen.
4. Paint the hair, facial features, and costume with glass stain. To prevent the colors from mingling, allow one color to dry before painting another color next to it.
5. Using the craft cement, glue the circle of construction paper to one side of the styrofoam ring. With the felt-tip pen, print a Hanukkah message on the paper.
6. Insert the stems of the flowers or leaves all around the styrofoam ring. Cement the decorated ring to one side of the doll. Let dry.
7. Clean the brush in solvent before storing.

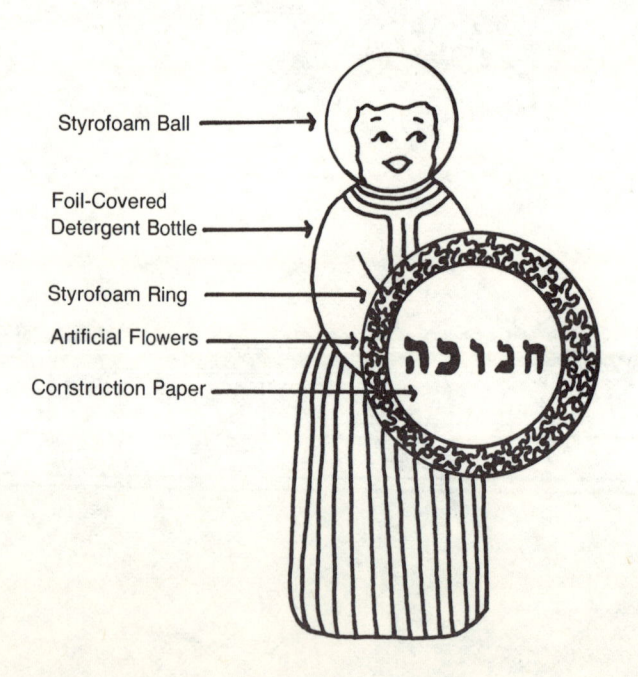

Set a Table

Let a beautifully set table be an invitation for friends and family to sit down and partake of traditional Hanukkah foods. From table coverings to centerpieces to a tray for serving potato pancakes (with the recipe on the tray), use the ideas in this section to help create a festive holiday mood.

Paper Cutout Tablecloth

Materials:

construction paper, 9" × 12", any colors
paper clip
pencil
scissors
white glue
white paper tablecloth

Method:

1. Choose three different colors of construction paper. Place on top of each other and clip together. Draw a large Hanukkah symbol on the top sheet and cut it out, going through all three layers. If the tablecloth is small, you may cut the colored paper in half before drawing the design.
2. Place the cutout designs on top of each other, so that each of the three layers shows (figure A). Glue in place.
3. Repeat steps 1 and 2 to make more cutouts.
4. Arrange the cutout designs, in their groups of three, on the paper tablecloth. Glue in a border around the edge of the cloth with a cluster in the center. The symbols in the center may be in a single layer, as shown in figure B.

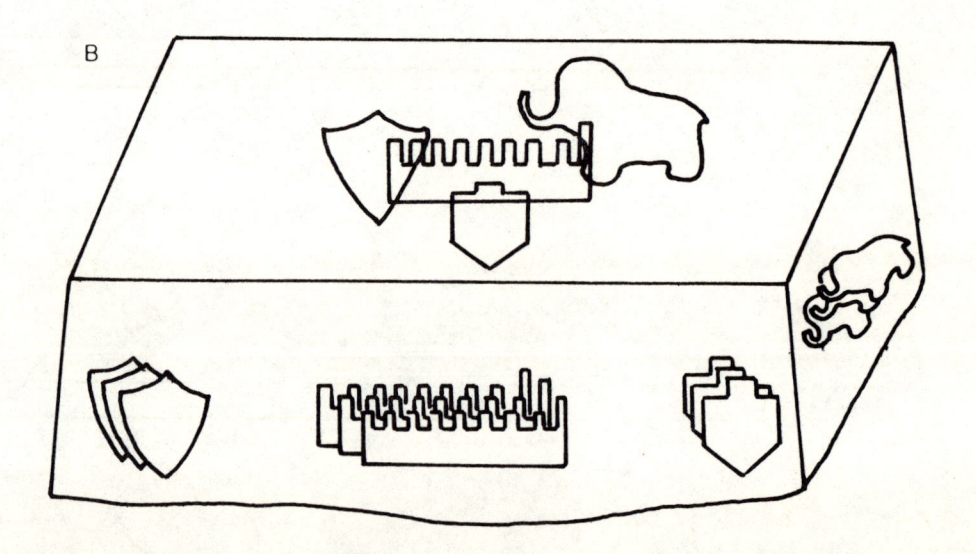

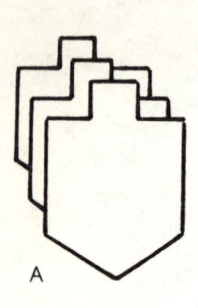

Bleach Out a Tablecloth Design

Materials:

denim fabric, dark color, size to fit your table
paper
pencil
1 sheet dressmaker's carbon paper, light color
newspapers
cold wax (from craft store)
2 brushes, one wide and one small
chlorine bleach
disposable container
rubber gloves
iron

Optional: needle, thread to match fabric

Method:
1. Wash the denim to remove any sizing. Let dry.
2. With a pencil, draw Hanukkah designs on the paper. Making one design at a time, place the dressmaker's carbon paper (it doesn't smear) face down on the material with your drawing over it. Trace over all the lines of your designs and remove the papers (figure A).
3. Place several layers of newspaper on the work surface. Spread out the fabric on the newspaper.
4. Using a wide brush for large areas and a small brush for details, brush cold wax inside all the designed areas. Let dry. Clean the brushes with water.
5. Use caution when working with bleach. Wear rubber gloves and try to

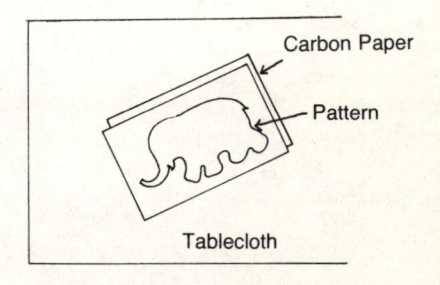

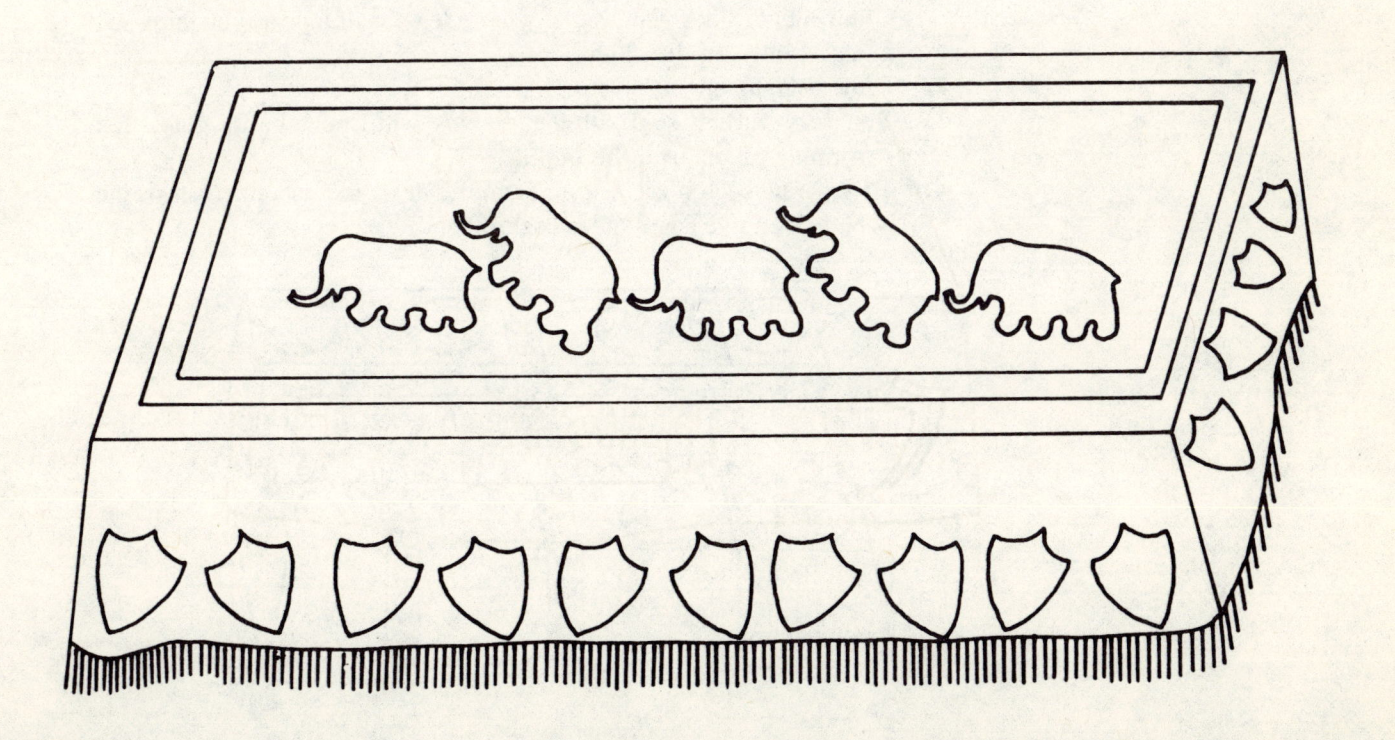

avoid splashing on skin and clothing. Mix one part bleach to one part water in the disposable container. Soak the fabric for 10 to 15 minutes. If you would like more of a bleached look, scoop out ½ cup of water, add it to another ½ cup of bleach, and pour the mixture back into the container.

6. To wash out the bleach, use cold running water or a large container of water. The fabric will lighten as it dries.
7. To absorb any wax that remains, iron the fabric between two layers of newspaper. Change the papers often, until no more wax comes off.
8. Fringe the fabric by pulling threads, one at a time, from the edges of the fabric to within one-half inch from each edge (figure B). Always pull the top thread first. The fabric may be hemmed instead, if you wish.

Tablecloth Runners

Materials:

roll of adding machine tape (from stationery store)
crayons, paint, or felt-tip pens

    Optional: tube of glue and glitter, any color (craft store)

Method:

1. Cut a length of tape to fit across the top of the tablecloth and extend down both sides. Cut as many more lengths of tape as you think will look pretty on the cloth.
2. Draw designs on each strip of tape.
3. You may outline some of the designs with the tube of glue, then sprinkle glitter over the outlines.
4. To separate each place setting from the next, the decorated strips can be woven over and under each other.

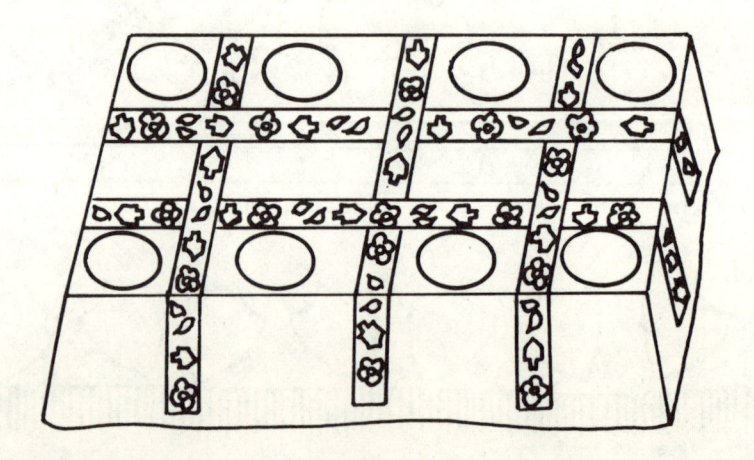

Plastic Covered Place Mats

Materials:

fabric (floral, gingham, polka dot, or striped) about 10″ × 15″ for each place mat

felt-tip pens, any color

clear, adhesive-backed paper, two 11″ × 16″ pieces for each place mat

Optional: pinking shears

Method:

1. Draw a design on the fabric. You may use the whole piece or cut around the outline of the design and discard the background.
2. Remove and discard the backing from one of the adhesive-backed papers and place the paper sticky side up on the table. Center the fabric over the paper and place it down, pressing firmly all over. Remove and discard the backing from the second sheet of paper and place the paper, centered, on top of the fabric. The two adhesive-backed papers should overlap the material and stick together.
3. Repeat steps 1 and 2 to make more place mats.
4. For a fancy border, trim the edges of the adhesive-backed paper with pinking shears.

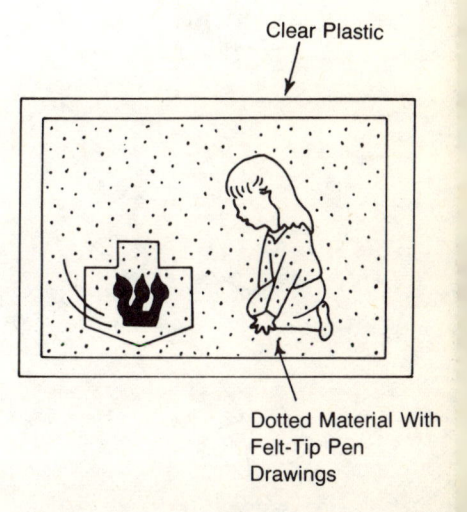

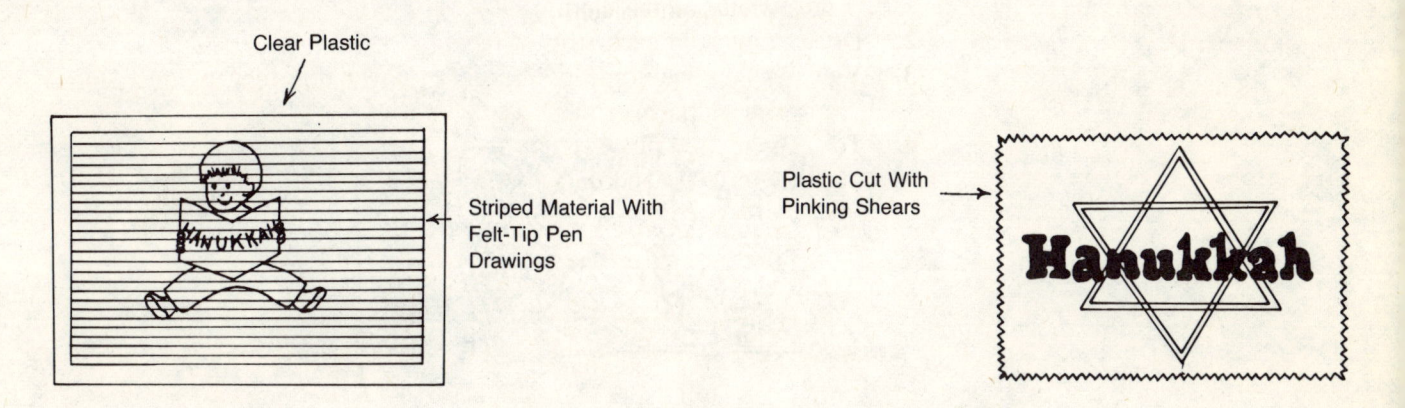

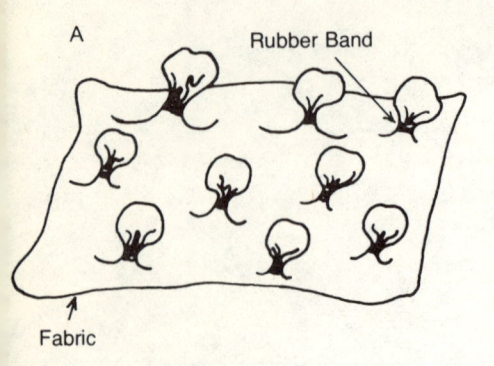

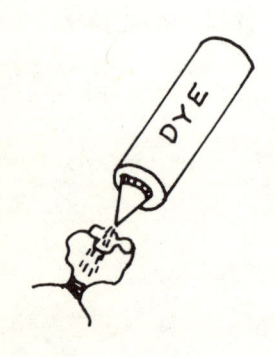

Tie-dyed Place Mats

Materials:

fabric (any washable material, but avoid polyesters and acrylics), about 10" × 15" for each place mat, white or light neutral color
newspapers
apron or old shirt
rubber bands
pencil
rubber gloves
liquid dye, any colors
squeeze bottle
iron

Method:

1. Wash the place mats to preshrink and remove sizing from the fabric. Wring out excess water.
2. Cover the work surface and the floor around the work area with newspapers. To prevent soiling clothes, wear an apron or old shirt.
3. At random, gather together sections of the wet place mat into "knots" and bind each section tightly with a rubber band (figure A).
4. Using a pencil, eraser side down, push down the center of each bound section until it reaches the rubber band (figure B).
5. Put on the rubber gloves, then pour the liquid dye into the squeeze bottle. Squeeze the dye into the well in the material formed by the pencil (figure C). A different color dye may be used for each well or for each place mat.
6. You may draw designs on the fabric around the knots (figure D).
7. Allow the dye to set for 15 to 20 minutes. Iron the place mat with the setting on medium.
8. Repeat steps 1–7 to make as many place mats as you like.
9. After using, the tie-dyed place mats can be washed by hand in cold water, without bleach.

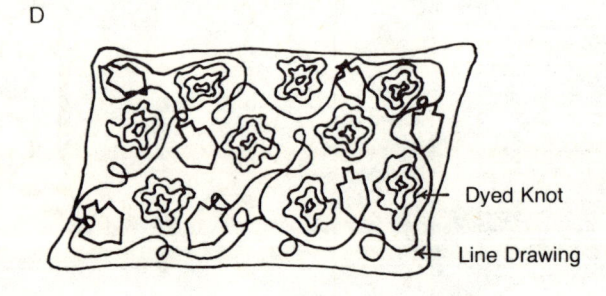

Holiday Napkin Holder

Materials:

corrugated cardboard (from carton) or thin wood, 8½" × 8½" (lumber yard or home supply center)
wrapping paper
white glue
wooden block, 2" × 4" (from child's block set, craft store, lumber yard, or home supply center)
yarn, any color
scissors
paper napkins with Hanukkah designs (Jewish bookstore or synagogue gift shop)

Method:

1. Wrap the cardboard with wrapping paper, as you would a gift. Glue the ends.
2. Wrap the wood block with wrapping paper and glue the ends.
3. With the glue, outline the word "Hanukkah," in Hebrew or English, on the wrapped block. Place cut lengths of yarn along the glued lines.
4. Place the wrapped board seam side down. Tie a length of yarn around the two opposite ends of the board, making bows on top.
5. Center a pile of napkins on the board between the bows. Place the "Hanukkah" block on the napkins to hold them down.

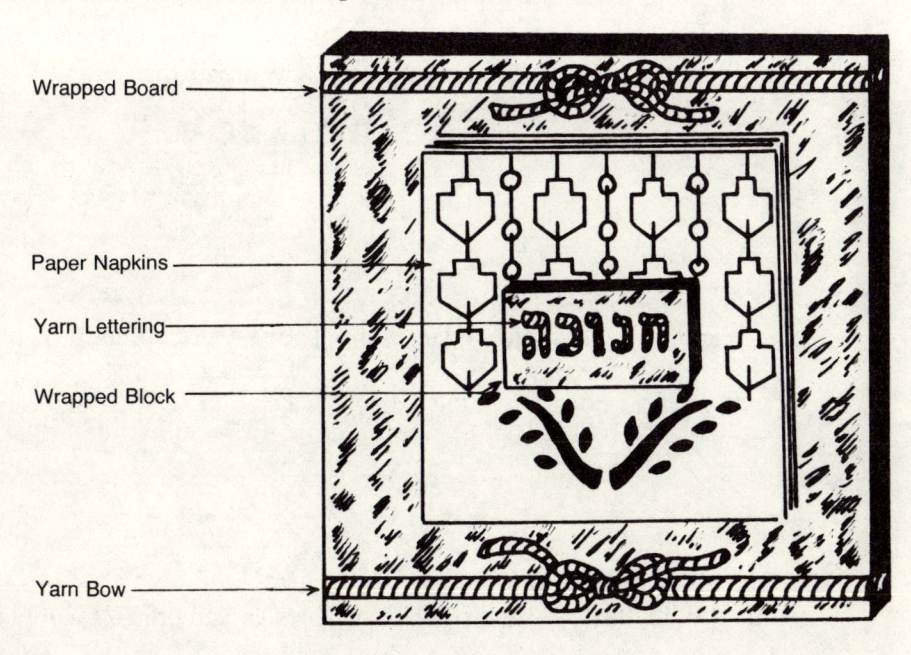

Napkin Rings

BURLAP NAPKIN RINGS

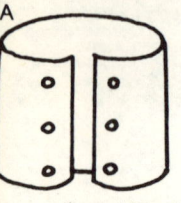

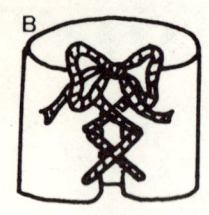

Start with a roll of burlap, 2½" wide (from craft store). To make one ring, cut a strip 2½" long.

Roll the strip, overlapping the two ends about ½ inch. Secure with white craft cement.

Glue on a sprig of artificial flowers (craft or variety store).

LACED PLASTIC NAPKIN RINGS

Start with an empty, clean plastic bleach bottle. To make one ring, use sharp scissors to cut a strip, 6½" long and 1½" wide.

With a hole punch, punch three holes on the two short ends of the strip (figure A).

Braid three lengths of yarn together. Use the braid to lace the ring together (figure B).

RIBBON-STRAW NAPKIN RINGS

Cut the tube from a roll of paper towels into 1-inch cylinders. Cut the ribbon straw (packaged from craft store) into an 8-foot length. To make one ring, wrap the ribbon around the cardboard cylinder, overlapping each strand. Continue until the entire ring is covered. Finish by gluing the end to the inside of the ring.

Burlap

Laced Plastic

Ribbon Straw

Picture-frame Recipe Tray

Materials:

frame with glass and a heavy cardboard backing, as large as you want the tray to be
white poster board to fit the frame
pencil
ruler
permanent marking pen, black
soft eraser
watercolor felt-tip pens; any colors

Method:

1. Remove the backing from the frame.
2. With the pencil and ruler, draw a design and print a favorite recipe on

the poster board. Potato latkes (pancakes) are a traditional Hanukkah food.
3. With the black pen, trace over all the penciled lines.
4. Erase any pencil lines that still show.
5. Paint the design with the watercolor pens. Because the black pen contains permanent ink, the watercolors may be painted over it without smearing.
6. Place the poster board in the frame and insert the backing firmly in place. Use to serve drinks, snacks, or whatever you have made using the recipe on the tray. The tray may be hung as a decoration when not in use.

Mosaic Tray

Materials:

metal or wood tray
mosaic tiles or decorative floor tiles each ½" square (from craft or variety store)
tile cement (craft store or home supply center)
dry grout or ready-mixed grout
disposable container
stick
spatula or squeegee
sponge
cloth

Method:

1. Arrange the tiles on the tray in a pleasing design, leaving small spaces between each tile for the grout.
2. Glue all the tiles down a small section at a time. Allow them to dry for 24 hours.
3. With a stick, mix the grout in the disposable container according to the directions on the package of grout.
4. Using the spatula or squeegee, spread the grout on the tray, working it into the spaces between the tiles. Wipe the excess off the top of the tiles.
5. When the grout is firm, clean the top of the tiles with a damp sponge. When completely dry, after 24 hours, polish the surface with a cloth.

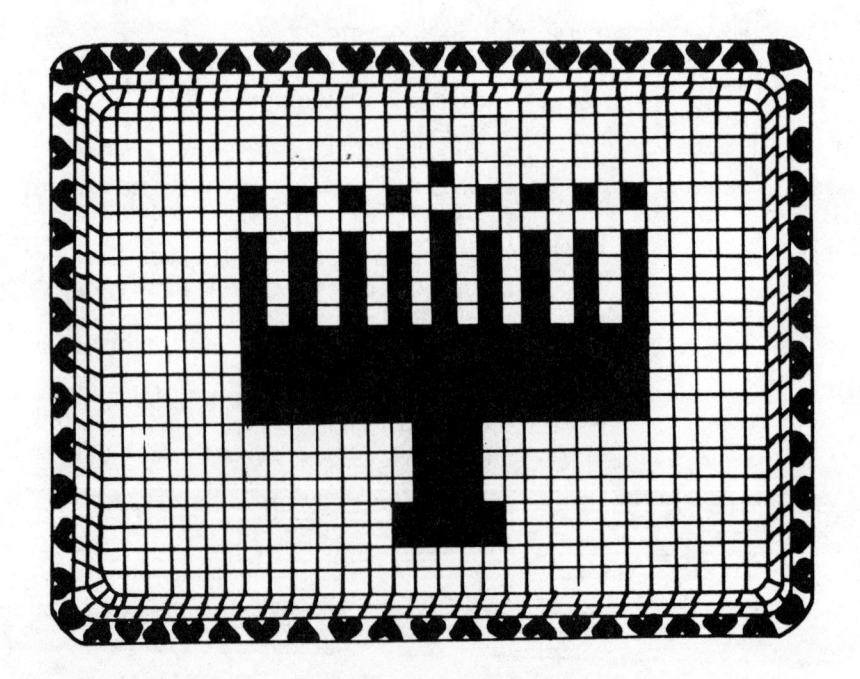

Have a Party

You will find projects in this section for having a party in your home, school, synagogue, or community center. To carry out a theme, you may wish to use the same decoration on the invitations, place cards, and party favors.

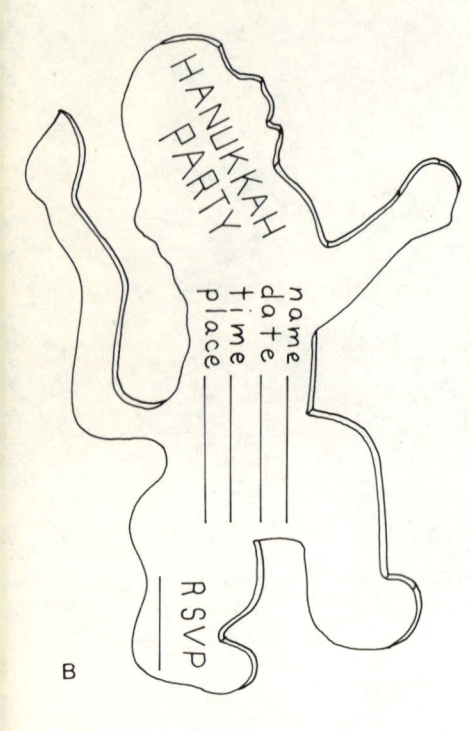

Foam Cutout Invitations

Materials:

1 sheet of lightweight cardboard
white styrofoam meat trays (from supermarket or butcher)
scissors
ball-point pen
envelopes, 3⅝" × 6½"

Method:

1. Cut the cardboard and styrofoam to fit inside one envelope. Each tray makes one invitation.
2. Draw a design on the cardboard and cut out (figure A).
3. Place the cardboard pattern on the styrofoam, trace around it with the pen, and cut it out.
4. With the pen, write information about the party on the styrofoam, as shown in Figure B.
5. Repeat steps 1–4 to make as many invitations as you need.
6. Insert each card in an envelope and send to your friends.

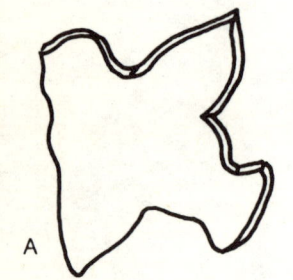

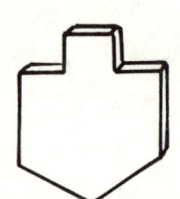

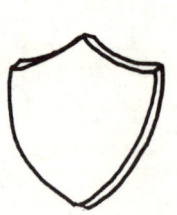

House-shaped Invitations

Materials:

sheets of paper, 3½" × 6"
pencil
ruler
scissors
glue
ball-point pen or felt-tip pen, any color
envelopes, 3⅝" × 6½"

Method:

1. Draw windows and a double door on one sheet of paper.
2. Cut around three sides of each window and up the center and across the top of the double door, as shown by the dotted lines in figure A.
3. Draw bricks or shingles on the house if you wish.
4. Glue the paper with the house drawn on it on top of a blank sheet of paper, but do not glue the windows and doors closed.
5. Write the information for the party in each window and door opening (figure B).
6. Repeat steps 1–5 to make as many invitations as you need.
7. Insert each card in an envelope and mail or deliver by hand.

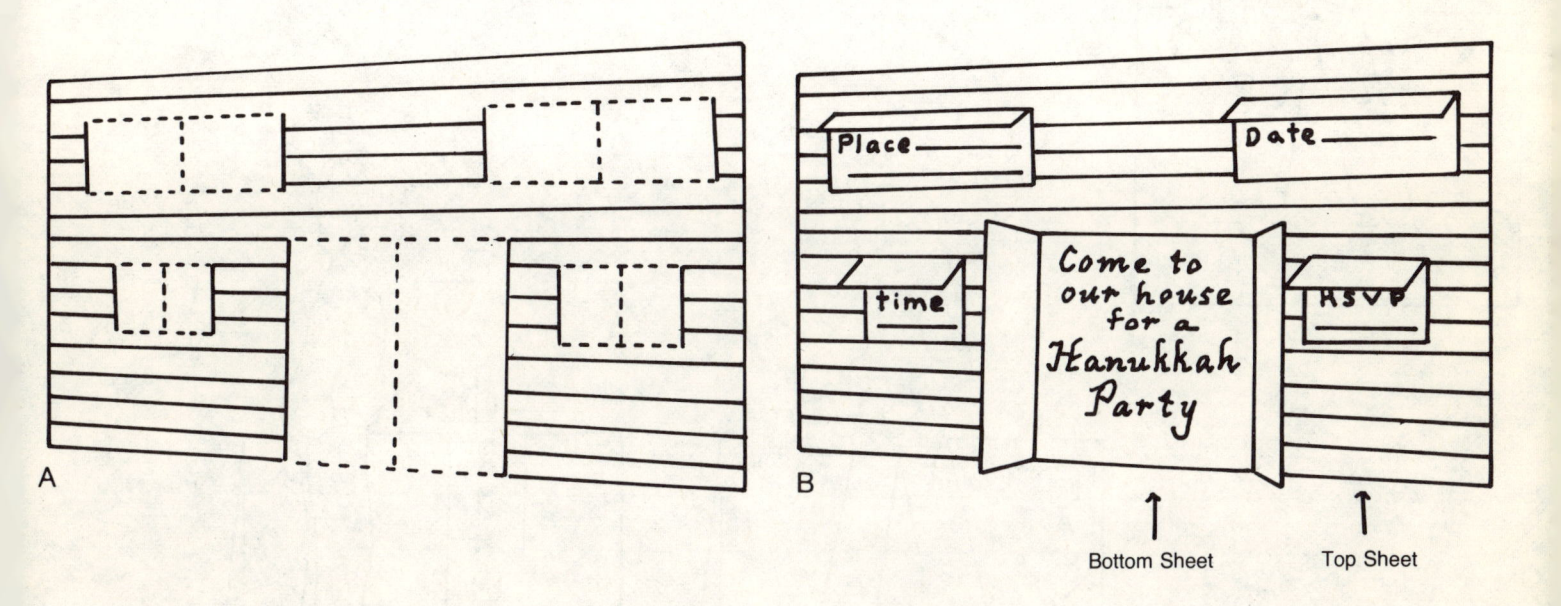

Place Cards

Materials:

sheets of poster board or heavy-duty drawing paper, 4½" × 6"
pencil
scissors
paint, felt-tip pens, or crayons

Method:
1. Draw a girl figure for each girl guest and a boy figure for each boy guest on the poster board. Make the figures almost the entire height of the card.
2. Draw a line across the center of the card, on both sides of the figure, as shown in figure A.
3. Cut up from the center line, following the outline of the top half of the figure, as shown by the dotted lines in figure B.
4. To make the figure stand, carefully fold back the paper around the top of the figure.
5. Write the name of one guest on each place card and decorate with paint, felt-tip pens, or crayons (figure C). Place on the party table.

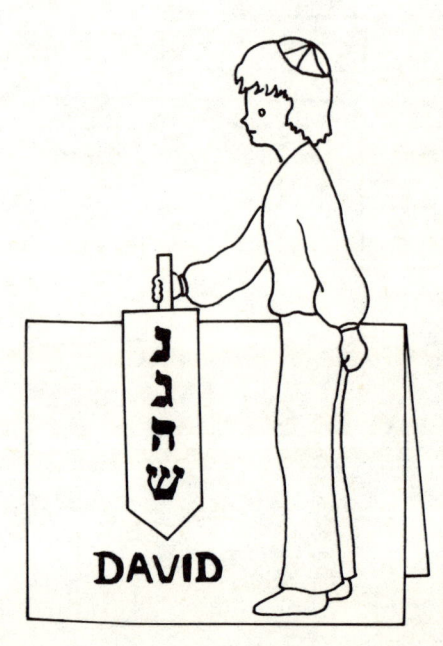

Place Marker and Party Favor

Materials:

construction paper
pencil
scissors
acrylic paint and brush or felt-tip pens, any colors

white glue
plastic drinking cups
chocolate Hanukkah *gelt* (coins) or other candy

Optional: ruler

Method:

1. To make one favor, draw a Hanukkah symbol on construction paper and cut it out.
2. Write the name of one guest on the symbol and decorate it.
3. Spread glue down the center of the back of the symbol. Attach the symbol to the plastic cup. Let dry.
4. Repeat steps 1–3 to make as many favors as you need.
5. Fill the cups with candy and place on the party table.

Back View

Dreidel Game Party Favor

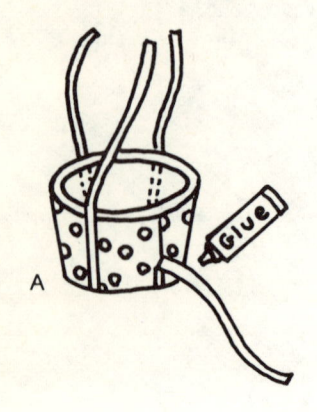

Materials:

small plastic container with lid (ice cream, margarine, or potato salad container)
measuring tape
fabric
scissors
white glue
ribbon
8 paper fasteners (from stationery or variety store)
dreidel
nuts, candy, or Hanukkah *gelt* (coins)

Optional: permanent felt-tip pens, any color

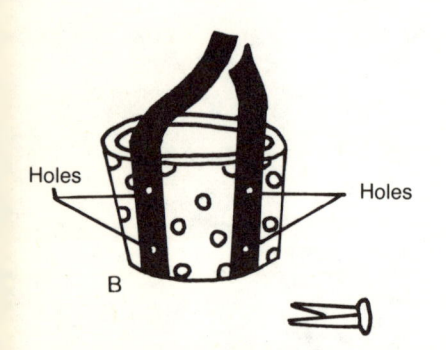

Method:
1. Measure the height of the container. Measure the circumference of the container and add one inch. Cut out the fabric to these measurements.
2. Cut the fabric width-wise into four sections.
3. Glue the fabric to the container, one section at a time.
4. Cut the ribbon into four lengths, leaving enough to extend and make "handles." Glue the ribbon to the container, covering the seams (figure A).
5. Carefully using the pointed end of the scissors, poke two holes through the ribbon, fabric, and container, one near the top and one near the bottom of the container (figure B). Insert a paper fastener into each hole. Do the same to the other three ribbons (figure B).
6. If the lid has printing on it, glue on a piece of fabric to cover the printing.
7. Cut a hole in the center of the lid, just large enough to pull the four ribbons through. Pull the ribbons through the hole and tie or knot the ends (figure C). The ribbon makes a handle for carrying the favor. The lid will slide up and down, but not fall off.
8. Put a dreidel in the container, then fill with candy, nuts, or Hanukkah *gelt*. Directions for playing the dreidel game are on page 27. You may print them on a sheet of paper to include with the dreidel party favor.

Beanbag Party Favor

Materials:

newspapers
pencil
scissors
fabric, cotton or felt
white craft cement
straight pins
needle and thread
decorative trim (from sewing or variety store)
candy
decorative safety pin (variety store)

Optional: paper, ribbon, plastic bags with ties, dried beans

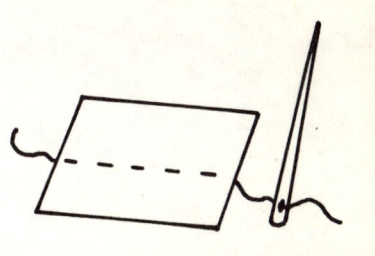

Method:
1. To make the pattern, draw a Hanukkah symbol on newspaper and cut it out.
2. To make one favor, place the newspaper pattern on the fabric and cut around it. Repeat to make two identical fabric cutouts.
3. Place the two cutouts together with the decorative sides facing in and pin together.
4. Sew all around the cutout, except around the top, in a small running or backstitch (figure A). Remove the pins.
5. Turn right side out. Glue decorative trim on one of the cutouts. Let dry. Fill with candy. Pin the top closed, going through both layers with the pin (figure B).
6. Repeat steps 1–5 to make as many favors as you need.
7. The guests may turn the party favors into beanbags. Tie a note to each favor with these directions on it: *To make a beanbag, remove the pin and the candy. Put dried beans in a plastic bag and tie closed, so the beans won't spill out if a seam opens. Sew the top closed with a small backhand stitch.*

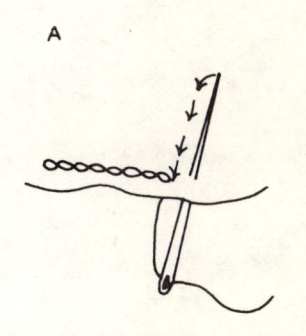

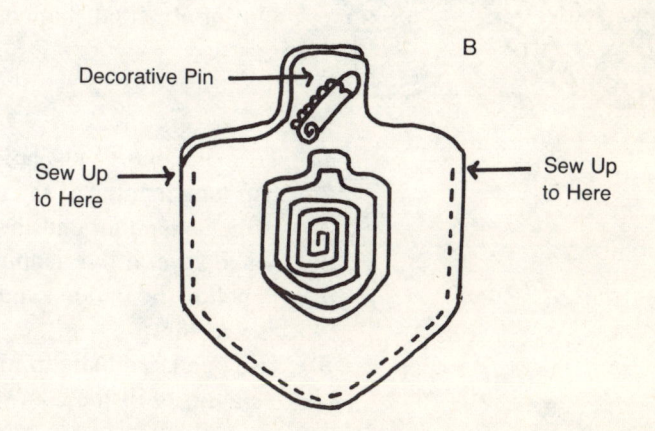

Paper Cup Candy Holders

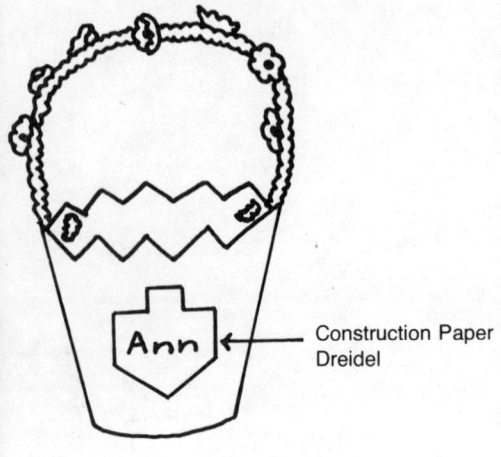

Materials:

plastic or paper drinking cups
scissors
hole punch
chenille pipe cleaners, any color
tiny artificial flowers (from craft store)
white glue
construction paper, any color
pencil
chocolate Hanukkah *gelt* (coins) or other candy

Construction Paper Dreidel

Method:
1. To make one favor, cut around the rim of the cup in a zigzag design.
2. Punch a hole on opposite sides of the top of the cup. Insert the pipe cleaner and bend the tips up to hold.
3. Twist the tiny flower stems around the pipe cleaner handle. If needed, attach with a drop of glue.
4. Draw a dreidel on construction paper to fit the cup and cut it out. Write the name of one guest on the dreidel. Glue the dreidel on the cup.
5. Repeat steps 1–4 to make as many favors as you need.
6. Fill the cups with candy and place on the party table.

Balloon Candy Holder

Materials:

1 large balloon
3-cord crochet (from craft store), any color
liquid starch
scissors
Hanukkah candies, wrapped

Optional: small balloons

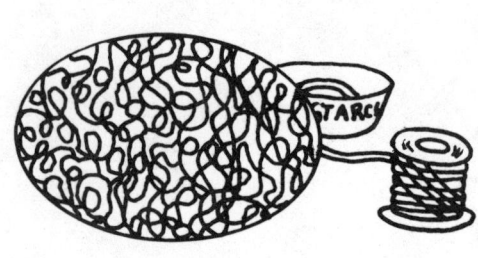

Method:
1. To make one candy holder, inflate a balloon and tie closed.
2. Dip long lengths of the cord crochet into the starch. Soak thoroughly, then drape around the balloon.
3. Make several overlapping layers of cord crochet. Let dry.
4. Puncture the balloon and remove it. Cut an opening in the cord crochet structure.
5. Use one large balloon for a centerpiece, or make several small ones as favors. Fill the candy holder with wrapped Hanukkah candies.

Tissue-twist Holder

Materials:

1 paper grocery bag
pencil
scissors
white glue
tissue paper, assorted colors
Hanukkah candy, cookies, or fruit

Method:

1. Draw a handle on the closed bag. Cut away part of the bag on both sides of the handle, as shown by the shaded area in figure A.
2. Open the bag. Overlap the ends of the handle and glue together (figure B).
3. Cut or tear the colored tissue paper into small pieces. Put your finger or the eraser end of the pencil in the center of a square, gathering the paper around your finger and pinching the bottom together (figure C). Dip your tissue-wrapped finger into the glue and press it in place on the bag. To make smaller tissue twists, use the end of a pencil instead of your finger.
4. Continue making twists until the bag is partly or completely covered (figure D).
5. Place on a table and fill with Hanukkah candy, cookies, or fruit.

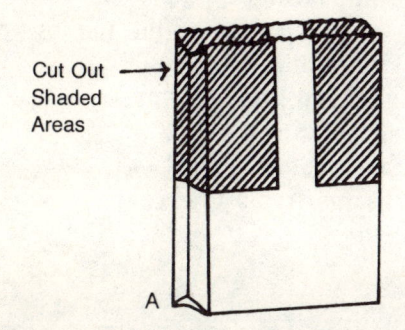

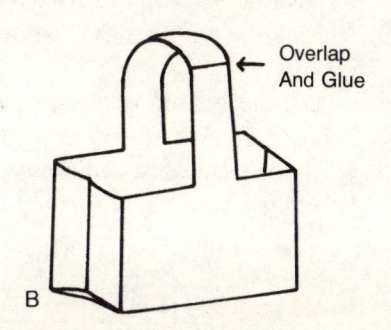

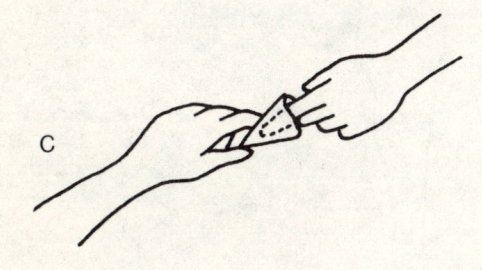

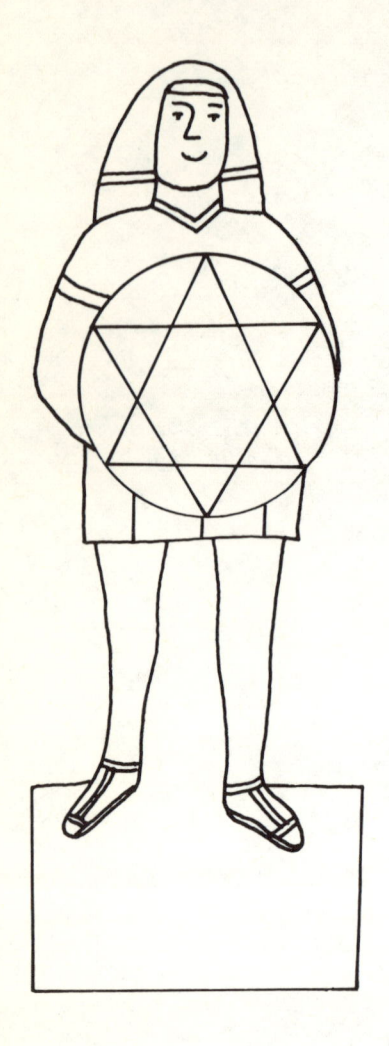

Maccabee Candy Holder

Materials:

1 piece of heavy cardboard, 6" × 12"
pencil
scissors
acrylic paint, any colors
fine brush
wide brush
1 piece of styrofoam, 8" in diameter, 1" thick (from craft store)
chocolate Hanukkah *gelt* (coins) or other candy
small dreidels, any colors

Optional: ribbon, 1" wide × 8½" long, any color, 5 decorative thumbtacks

Method:

1. To make the cardboard pattern, draw a Maccabee figure standing on a small square, as shown in figure A. Cut it out.
2. Place the pattern on another section of the cardboard, trace around the outline, and cut out.
3. Repeat step 2 to make a total of five figures.
4. Decorate each figure with paint, using the fine brush.
5. Using the wide brush, paint one side of the styrofoam and its rim. Let dry.
6. Push the bottom of each figure into the styrofoam base.
7. You may tack ribbon around the rim of the styrofoam.
8. Fill the Maccabee centerpiece with candy and dreidels. The five Maccabee brothers will stand guard over it (figure B).

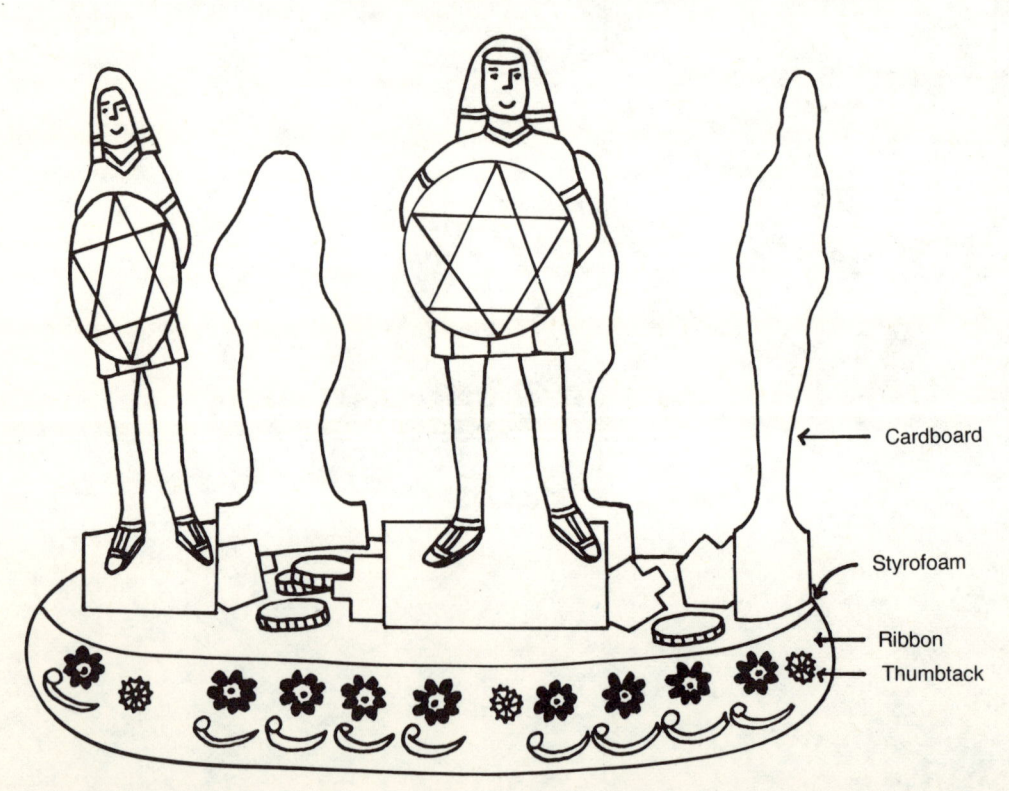

Play a Game

From days of old, it has been a custom for Jews to play games of chance during Hanukkah. Traditionally, women do no work while the candles are burning in the menorah (at least half an hour). This is a good time for family and friends to play dreidel together. Make and play some of the games in this section. Give some of the games as gifts or store them from year to year for get-togethers and parties.

Get the Latkes in the Oven

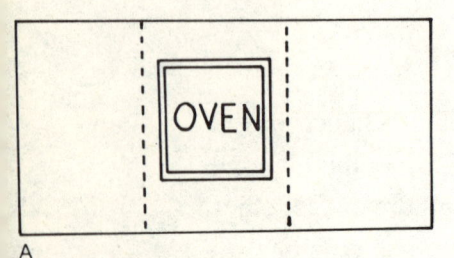

Materials:

poster board or oak tag, about 22" × 28"
scissors
pencil
masking tape
straws

Optional: construction paper, crayons, paint, or felt-tip pens

Method:

1. Cut the sheet of poster board or oak tag in half lengthwise or tape sheets of construction paper together.
2. Fold one of the halves into thirds and unfold.
3. Write the word "oven" in large letters in the center section (figure A).
4. Decorate the end sections if you wish. Adjust the end sections so the "oven" can stand (figure B).
5. Draw "latkes," one for each player, on the remaining half of the poster board. Cut out.
6. With the masking tape, mark a starting line on the floor.
7. To play, kneel on your hands and knees. Each player puts a straw in his or her mouth. Using only the straw—no hands—the first player to blow a latke into the oven wins.

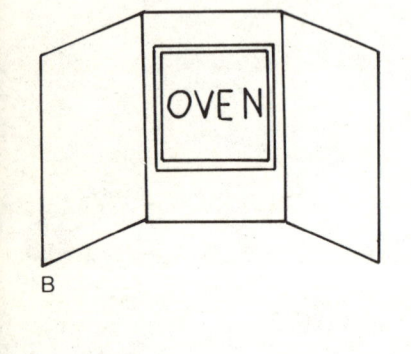

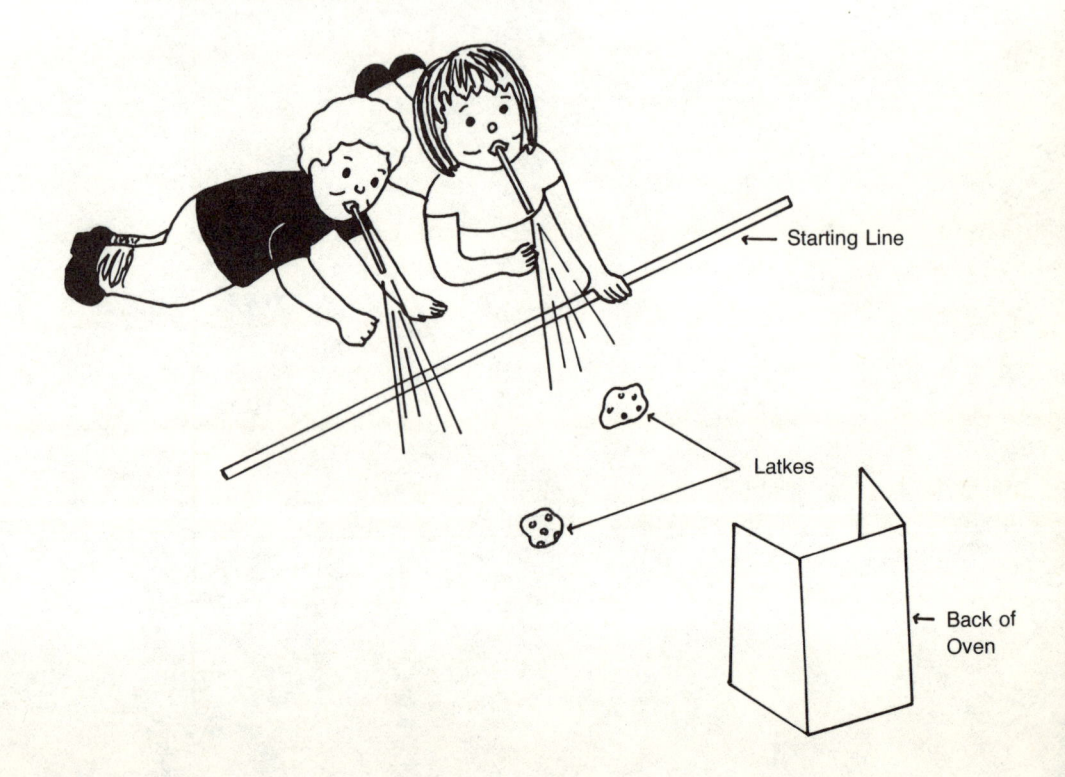

Light-the-menorah Game

Draw a menorah on heavy cardboard and cut it out. Decorate with paint or felt-tip pens. Glue the decorated menorah to a shallow box.

Use nine metal or rubber washers as "flames." Standing about one foot away, a player must first ring the *shamash* with a "flame," then try to "light" the other candles. After he has tossed all of his "flames," count the "lit" candles and remove the washers.

The next player takes a turn. The player who "lights" the most candles wins the game.

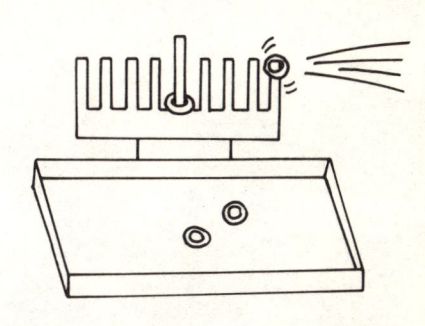

Pin the Shield on Judah Maccabee

On a large sheet of paper or a cut-open paper bag, draw the picture shown in figure A. Do the same for figure B. Cut out the shield (figure B) and use it as a pattern to make one shield for each player.

Color the shields and the picture of Judah Maccabee. Write a player's name on each shield. Put a piece of tape, sticky side down, on each shield.

To play, one player at a time is blindfolded and tries to tape the shield in the right place. The player whose shield is closest wins the game.

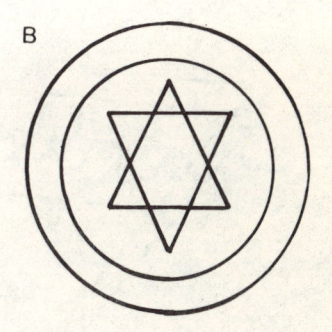

Hanukkah Hop Game

Materials:

denim, or other sturdy fabric, 2′ wide × 5′ long, any color
pencil
ruler

acrylic paint, any color
soft brush
checker, bottle cap, or stone
box

Optional: box or bag

Method:

1. To make the game mat, draw eight squares, 12″ each, on the fabric.
2. Paint on the lettering and numbers, as shown below. Let dry.
3. To play, stand at the foot of the mat and toss the checker onto the first square, labeled "Hanukkah." On one foot, hop onto number 1, bend down, pick up the checker, and hop off the mat. If you did this without putting your other foot down, you may toss the checker onto the second square. Continue until you have successfully hopped on and off all eight squares.

    If the checker lands in the wrong box or if your other foot touches the ground, you are "out." The next player takes a turn. When it is your turn again, you may start with the number you last completed.
4. The game mat may be washed by hand or by machine on gentle cycle, in cold water, with no bleach. To store the game from year to year, fold or roll the mat and place in a box or bag.

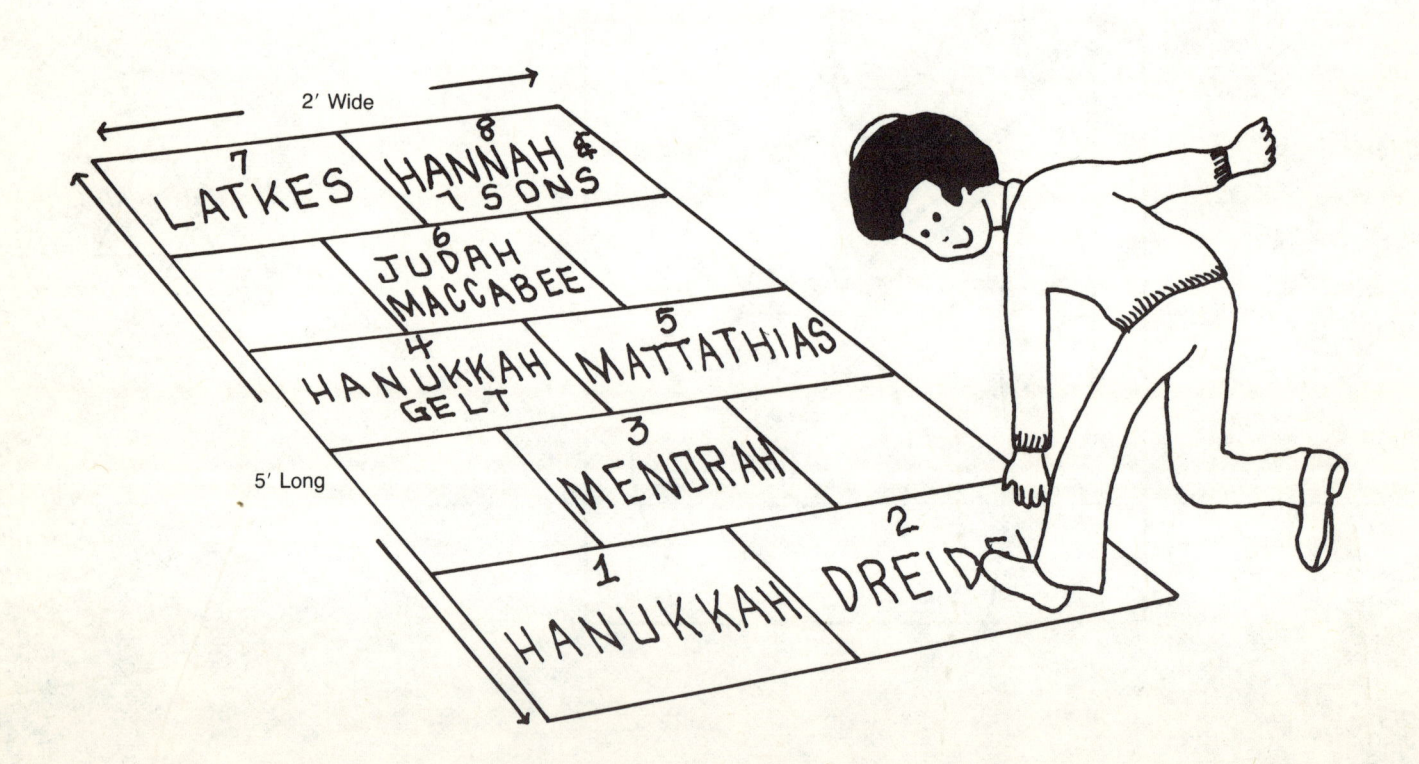

Dreidel Nut Toss

Materials:

1 cardboard box, at least 8" square
ruler
scissors or craft knife
pencil
paint and brush or felt-tip pens, any colors
masking tape
whole nuts in their shells, 6 for each player

Optional: craft knife

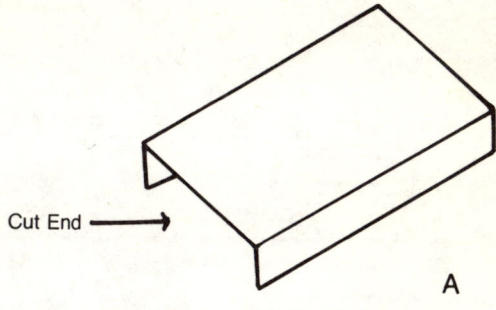

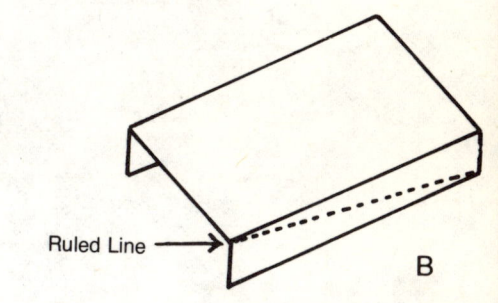

Method:

1. Cut off one of the short ends of the box as shown in figure A.
2. Rule a diagonal line from the top of the cut end to the bottom of the closed end on both long sides of the box (figure B).
3. Cut along the ruled lines. The box is now slanted (figure C).
4. Draw 6 dreidels with circles inside (figure D). Cut out each circle using scissors or the craft knife. Decorate the box with paint or felt-tip pens.
5. With the tape, mark a tossing line on the floor. Place the box about 3' to 5' away.
6. To play, give each player 6 nuts. The first player stands in back of the tossing line and tosses or rolls all of his nuts, one at a time, aiming at the hole marked with the highest number. Each person adds up his own score as the game is played. If a nut lands in the hole marked ''out,'' the player's turn is over. The player with the highest score wins the game.

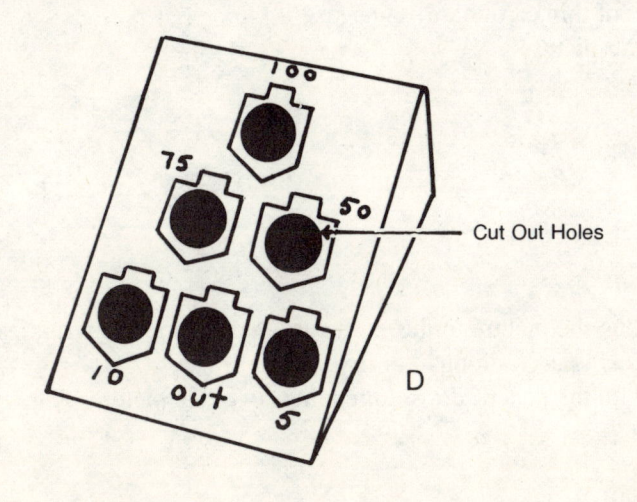

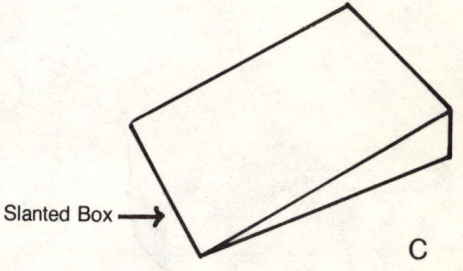

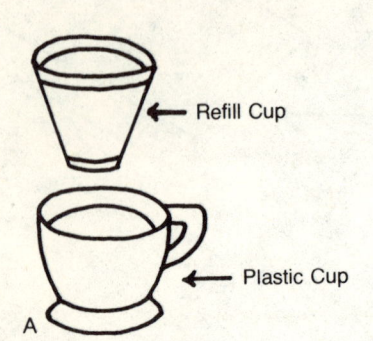

Ball-in-the-dreidel Cup Game

Refill Cup
Plastic Cup
A

ש ה ג נ
B

Knot
Knot
C

Materials:

1 refill cup for plastic coffee cup container (from supermarket or department store)
permanent felt-tip pens, any colors
yarn, 15" long
heavy-duty needle
small styrofoam ball (craft store)

Method:

1. Decorate the refill cup (figure A) with the pens. Add the Hebrew letters (figure B) around the cup.
2. Thread the needle with the yarn. Poke it through the styrofoam ball. Knot one end of the yarn.
3. Pull the needle through the rim of the cup. Remove the needle and knot the end of the yarn (figure C).
4. To play, hold the cup in one hand and toss the ball into the cup. The player who gets the ball into the cup with the fewest tries wins. Keep practicing—beat your own record.

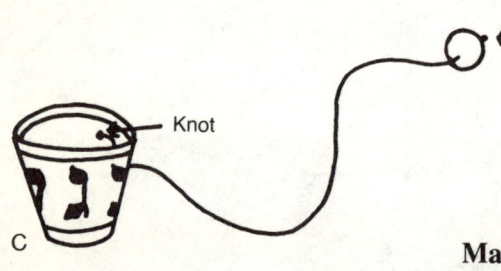

Cut-and-paste Puzzle

Materials:

picture cut from Hanukkah workbook, coloring book, magazine, or card
1 sheet of thin cardboard, same size as the picture
white glue
pencil
scissors
box

Method:

1. Glue the picture to the cardboard, smoothing out wrinkles in the paper as you go along. Let dry.
2. With the pencil, draw dotted lines over the picture. A few lines make a

simple puzzle; more lines make a more complicated puzzle.
3. Cut along the dotted lines. Place the pieces in the box when not using so they won't get lost.

Dreidel Spinner

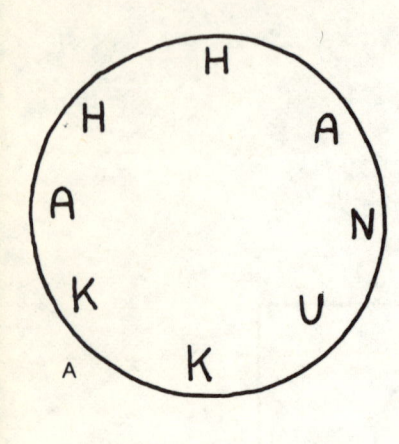

Materials:

2 round paper plates, each 9" diameter
pencils, 1 for each player
felt-tip pens, any colors
ruler
scissors
1 paper fastener
sheets of paper, 1 for each player

Method:

1. With a pencil, write the word "Hanukkah," evenly spaced, around the rim of one of the plates. When you are satisfied with the letter spacing, write over each letter with a felt-tip pen (figure A).
2. To make the spinner, draw a dreidel on the second plate (figure B).
3. Cut out the dreidel. Decorate with the pens.
4. Poke a hole through the center of the dreidel and the center of the lettered plate. Fasten together with the paper fastener (figure C).
5. The word "Hanukkah" is written on each piece of paper. To play the game, each person takes a turn spinning the dreidel. The letters must be spun in proper spelling order. When the spinner stops at the proper letter, that letter gets circled on the paper. The first person who completes the circling of the letters in the word "Hanukkah" wins.

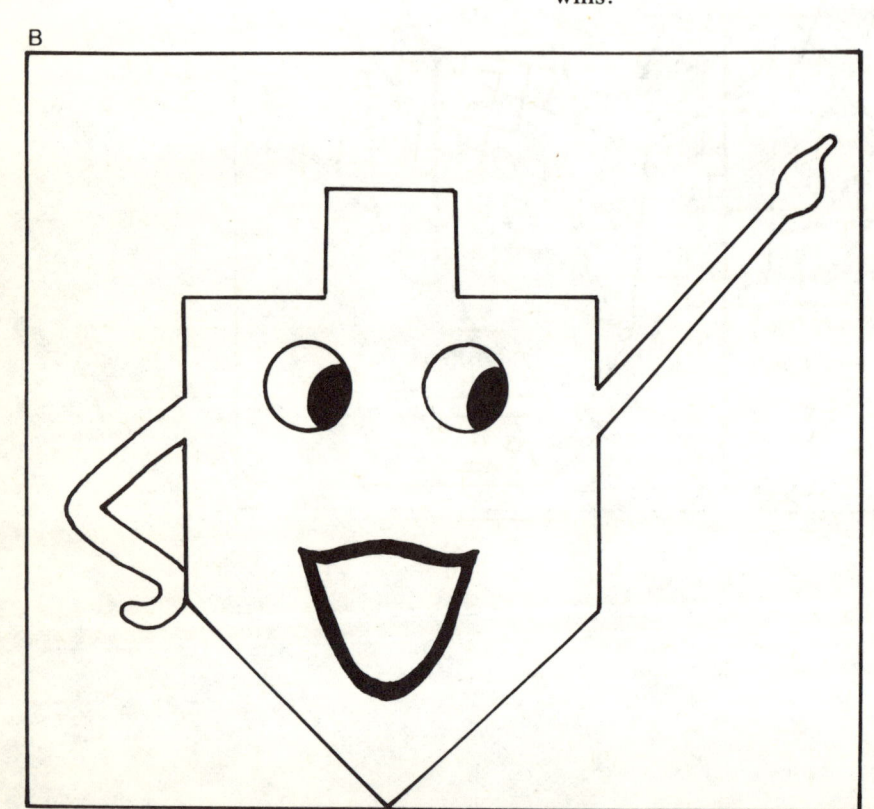

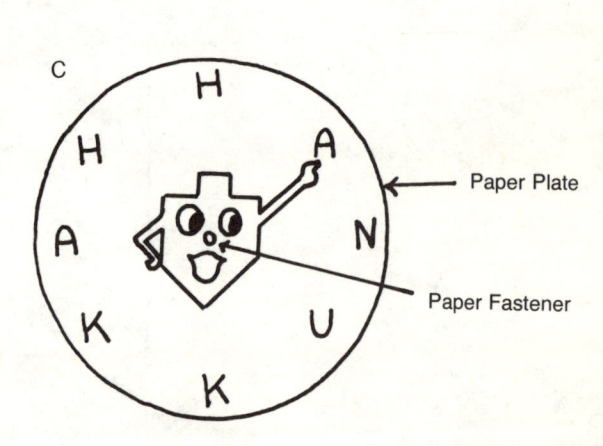

Hanukkah Word Game

With a pencil or pen, draw a square containing 36 smaller squares on each sheet of a pad of paper (figure A). Tear off one sheet and cut out the squares. In each square, print one letter from each of these words (figure B): DREIDEL, HANUKKAH, LATKES, MACCABEE, MENORAH.

Place the pad, lettered squares, and several pencils in a decorated box (figure C). On the inside of the box lid, write these directions for playing the game:

Place the lettered squares in a container. One person calls out one letter at a time. The total number of letters in the words (36) equals the 36 squares on each sheet of paper. The other players write the letter in any square they think will help make a word. The words may be formed horizontally or vertically. After all the letters are called, the player who has made the most words wins the game.

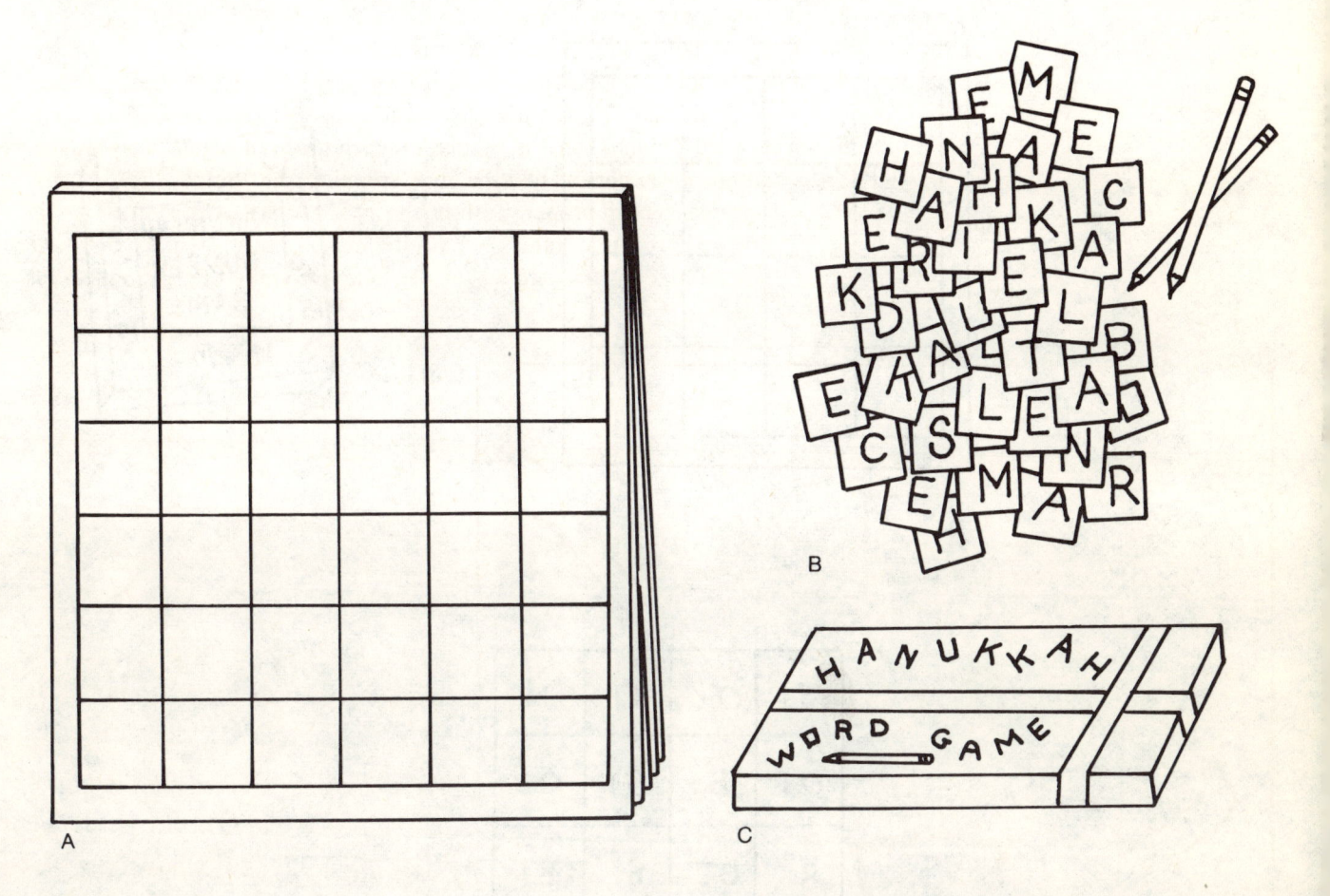

Hanukkah Number Game

With a pencil or pen, draw a square containing 16 smaller squares on each sheet of a pad of paper (figure A). Tie a ribbon around the pad. Tuck several pencils into the ribbon and place in a decorated box (figure B).

On the inside of the box lid, write these directions for playing the game (print the answer upside down):

Each player gets one sheet of paper. Each player should write one of the numbers below in each square. If arranged properly, the numbers in each row across and each row down will add up to 44. This is the total number of candles lit on the 8 nights of Hanukkah.
3 5 8 9 10 10 10 10 11 11 12 13 14 15 15 20
Turn right side up for the correct answer.

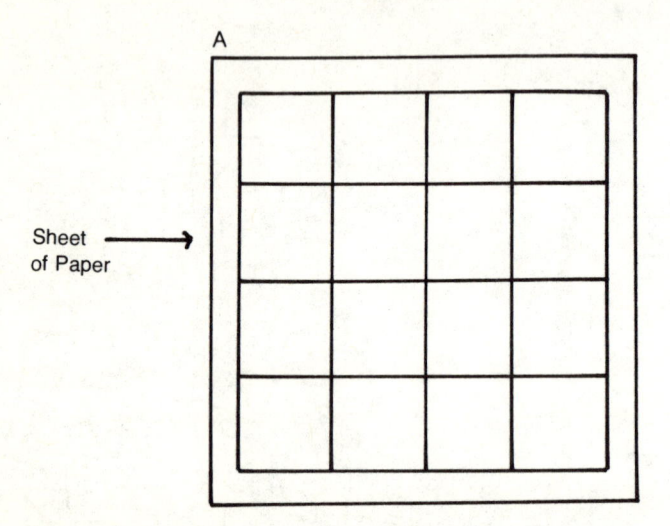

ANSWER

10	15	5	14
13	3	20	8
10	15	9	10
11	11	10	12

Put on a Show

Plays, puppet shows, readings, songs, and dances are enjoyable ways to teach and learn about Hanukkah.

Put on a play or puppet show for home celebrations or classroom parties. Ideas for costumes and staging are in this section.

Costumes for a Hanukkah Play

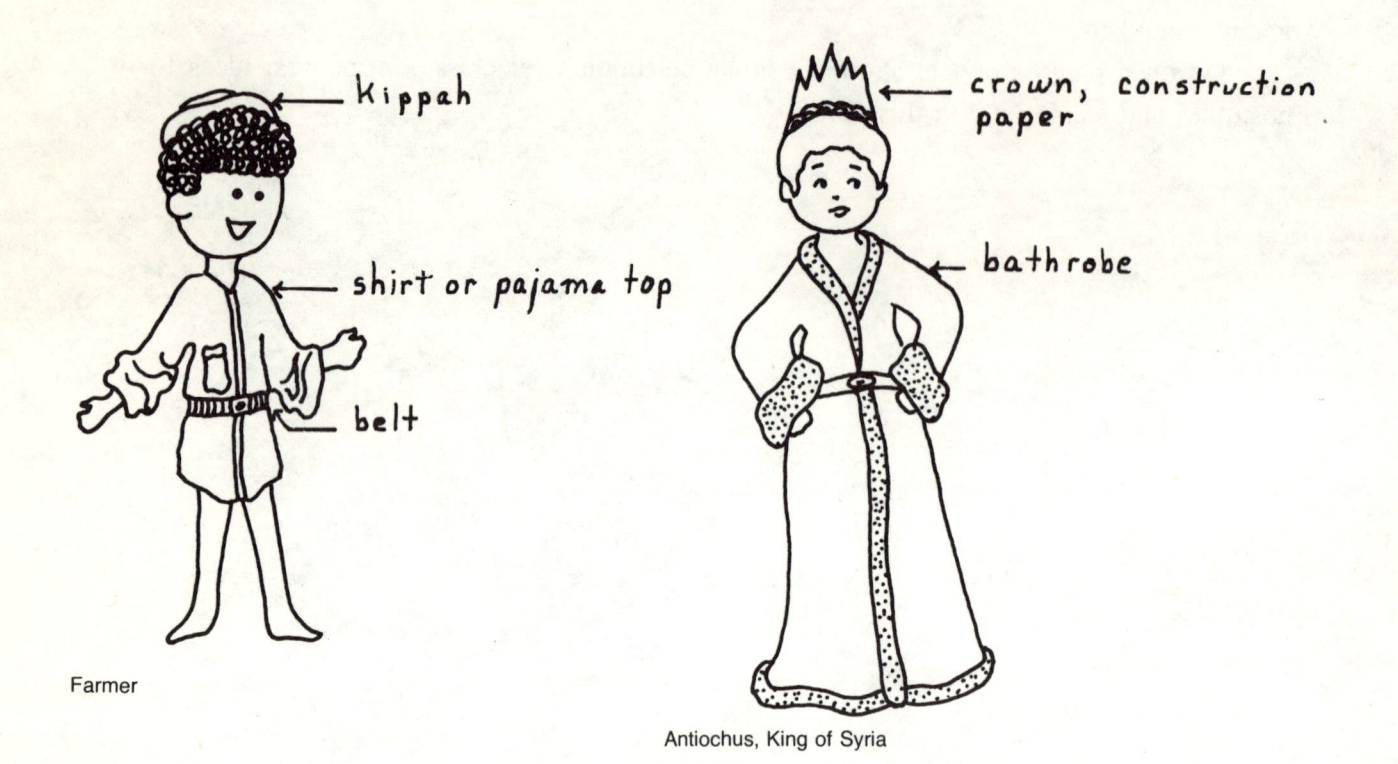

- kippah
- shirt or pajama top
- belt

Farmer

- crown, construction paper
- bathrobe

Antiochus, King of Syria

- kippah
- polo shirt
- cloth or crepe-paper skirt
- foil-covered cardboard sword
- sandals with laces
- heavy cardboard circle or garbage pail cover with painted or colored cloth tape symbol

Judah Maccabee

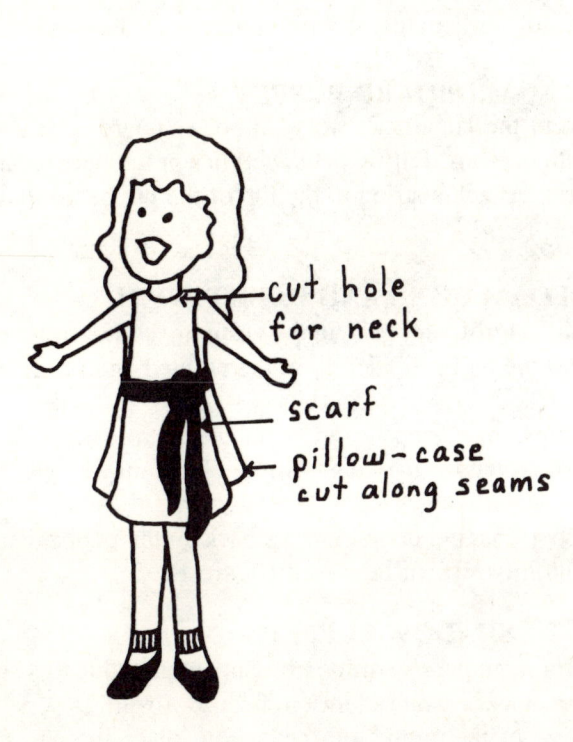

Child
- cut hole for neck
- scarf
- pillow-case cut along seams

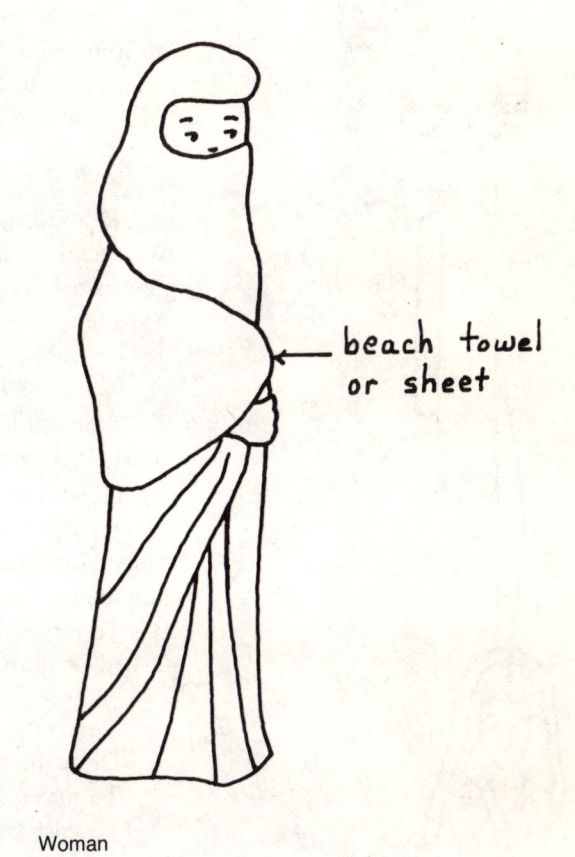

Woman
- beach towel or sheet

Hellenist
- Greek key on fabric or paper – design is painted or glued-on yarn
- robe, housedress, or tablecloth

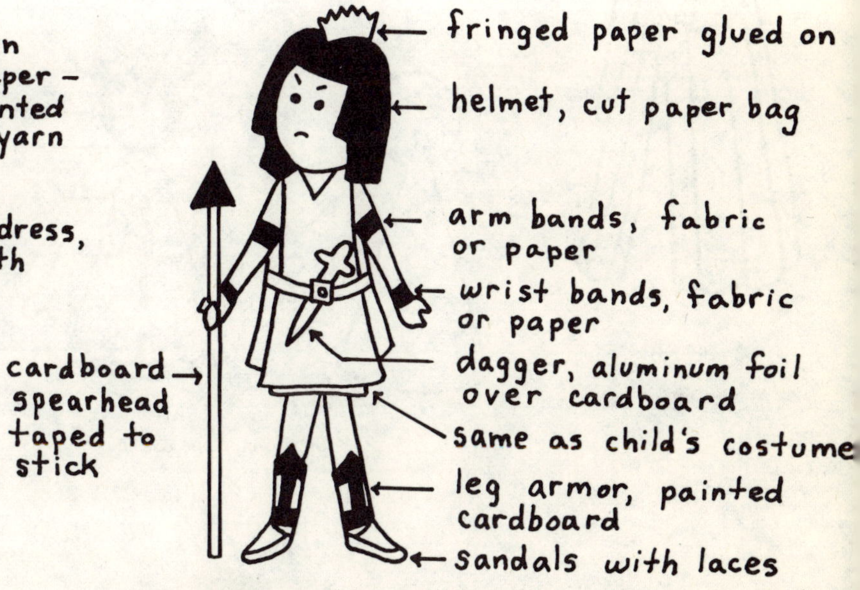

Syrian Soldier
- fringed paper glued on
- helmet, cut paper bag
- arm bands, fabric or paper
- wrist bands, fabric or paper
- dagger, aluminum foil over cardboard
- same as child's costume
- leg armor, painted cardboard
- sandals with laces
- cardboard spearhead taped to stick

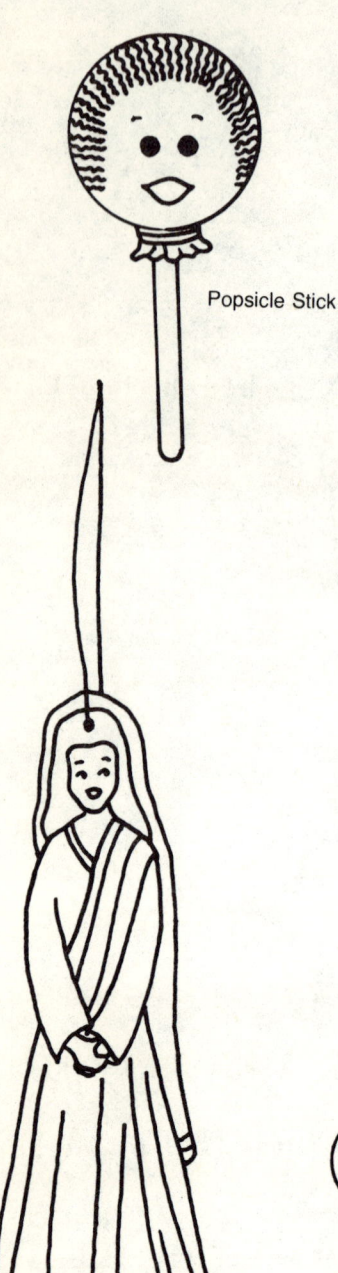

POPSICLE STICK PUPPET

Place a ball of cotton over one end of a popsicle stick. Cover it with fabric or a cutoff sock. Secure the bottom with a rubber band.

Add features with permanent felt-tip pens or fabric markers. To make hair, eyebrows, or beard, cut lengths of yarn and glue to the head.

CARDBOARD PUPPET

Draw a figure from the Hanukkah story on poster board. Cut it out. Add facial features with crayons, felt-tip pens, acrylics or tempera paint, or glue on scraps of fabric. Attach a string to the top of the puppet to make it move.

STYROFOAM CONE AND BALL PUPPET

Start with a small styrofoam ball and styrofoam cone (from craft store). Poke a hole into the ball and stick it on the pointed end of the cone (figure A).

Paint facial features, hair, and costume on the styrofoam with acrylics. Add a cardboard crown for the king. A little object may be glued on the painted hands.

To move the puppet, insert a dowel into its back so the puppet can be pushed or into the bottom so it can be raised (figure B).

SHADOW PUPPET

Draw the figure for a puppet on cardboard. Cut out and glue to a stick. To make a screen, tack a white cloth or sheet to a wall.

To cast the shadow of the puppet on the screen, place the puppet in front of a strong light from a projector, lamp, or flashlight. Move the puppet by using the stick as a handle.

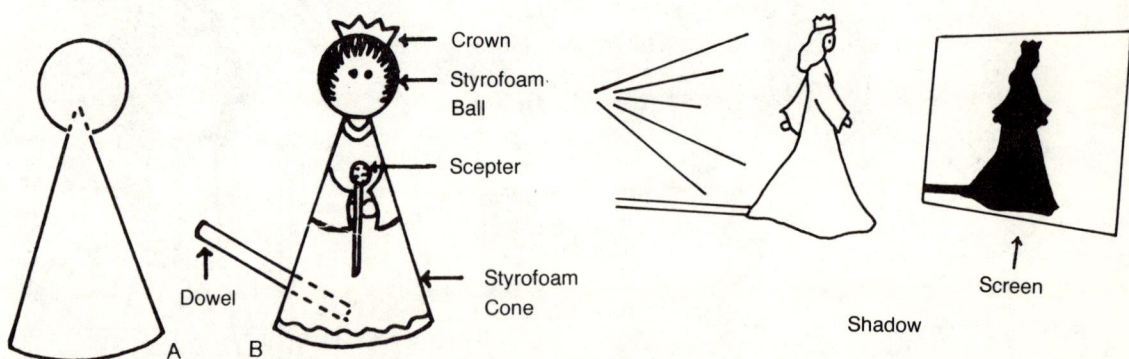

CLOTHESPIN PUPPET

Place a tissue or old handkerchief over the head of a clothespin. Secure by wrapping a pipe cleaner around the base of the clothespin head (figure A). To make the hands, curve the ends of the pipe cleaner forward.

Trim the bottom of the skirt with scissors. Use the scraps to make a headdress and glue on (figure B). Draw eyes, mouth, and fringes of hair with a felt-tip pen.

To move the puppet, insert a stick into the back of the clothespin and push the puppet back and forth (figure C).

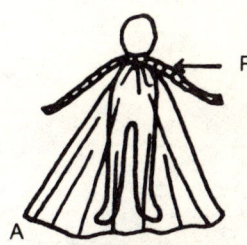

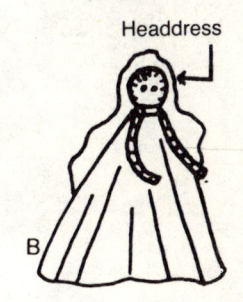

MODELED HEAD PUPPET

Shape a puppet head from clay or instant papier-mâché. Decorate with paint or paper cutouts.

Roll a strip of cardboard into a ring shape and tape closed (figure A). To make the neck, push the cardboard roll into the clay.

Cut out and sew together two identical paper or cloth costumes. Do not sew bottom, neck, or hand holes (figure B). Glue the costume to the collar.

To move the puppet, insert your forefinger in the head and your middle finger and thumb in the arms (figure C).

RAG DOLL ROD PUPPET

With white craft cement, attach a thin wooden dowel to the underside of a soft rag doll. Attach another dowel to each of the doll's hands.

Decorate the doll to look like one of the Hanukkah characters with scraps of fabric glued on with white craft cement.

To move the puppet, hold the bottom rod in one hand and the two hand rods in your other hand.

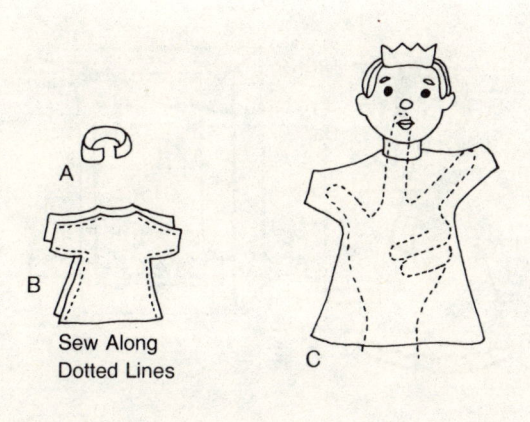

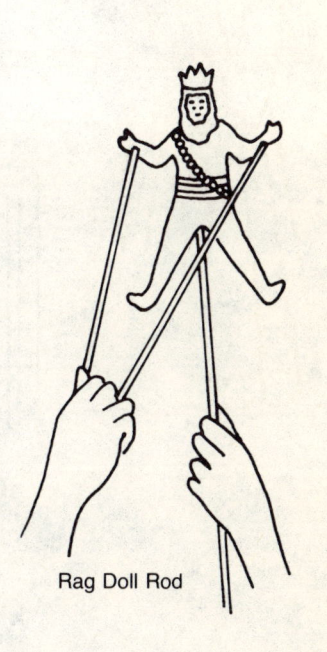

Movies

SHOE BOX MOVIE THEATER

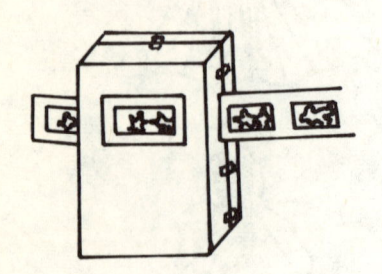

Cut a window in the bottom of a shoe box or any small box. Cut slits in the sides of the box the same length as the window. (The slits should start and end in line with the window.) Tape the cover on and decorate the outside of the box with crayon, paint, or glued-on colored paper or fabric. Make pictures telling the story of Hanukkah and glue them in order on a long strip of paper. (Leave about 1" between each picture.) Insert the strip in one slit, then push it through the box and out through the other slit. To put on a show, slowly pull the strip as each picture shows through the window. Store the picture story in the box after the show is completed.

CARDBOARD BOX MOVIE THEATER

Stand a box on end and tape the cover to the box. With a knife, slit the cover down the center and fold back each side. Make holes on the top and bottom of each side of the box. Illustrate a long roll of paper with pictures from the Hanukkah story and print excerpts from the text. Insert the cardboard tubes from two rolls of paper towels through the top and bottom holes. Glue the beginning of the paper strip to the top tube and the end of the strip to the bottom tube. Decorate the outside of the box with poster paint. Open the doors to show the movie and close them when finished. You may glue a tiny cork on each door as a handle.

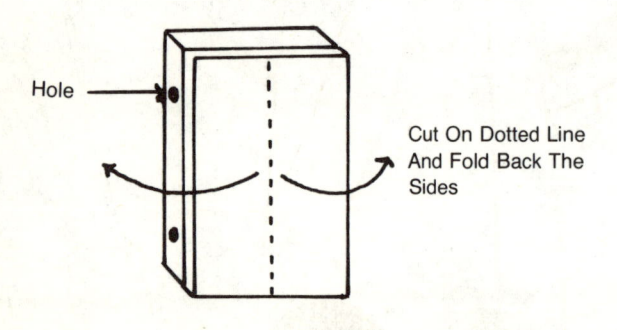

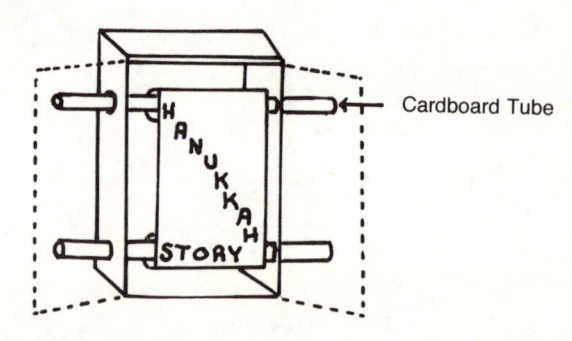

Puppets

FINGER PUPPETS

On lightweight cardboard or heavy paper, draw Hanukkah characters in pencil.

To make the legs, cut two holes with small, sharp scissors (manicure). One hole should fit your forefinger; the other should fit your middle finger.

Decorate the cutout figures with crayons, paint, or felt-tip pens. Wiggle your fingers to move the puppets.

Mattathias

Hannah

Hanukkah Gelt

Hanukkah Song

Dreidel

Finger Puppets

Puppet Theaters

CARDBOARD BOX STAGE

Remove the top flaps from a large cardboard box. For stage openings, cut a large hole in front of the carton and smaller holes in the sides and back. These openings enable the puppets to enter the stage from either side, the back, or the top of the "stage." Paint the outside and paint scenery on the back wall.

SHADOW PUPPET STAGE

Remove the top flaps from a shallow carton and place it on a table with the opening facing the audience. Cut away the back of the carton. Stretch thin fabric or tissue paper across the opening that faces the audience and glue down.

Place a strong light (from a spot lamp, projector, or flashlight) behind the carton, directed toward the screen. Place the puppet close to the screen in the path of the light as the shadow is cast on the screen. Or manipulate the puppet through a slit in the side of the carton.

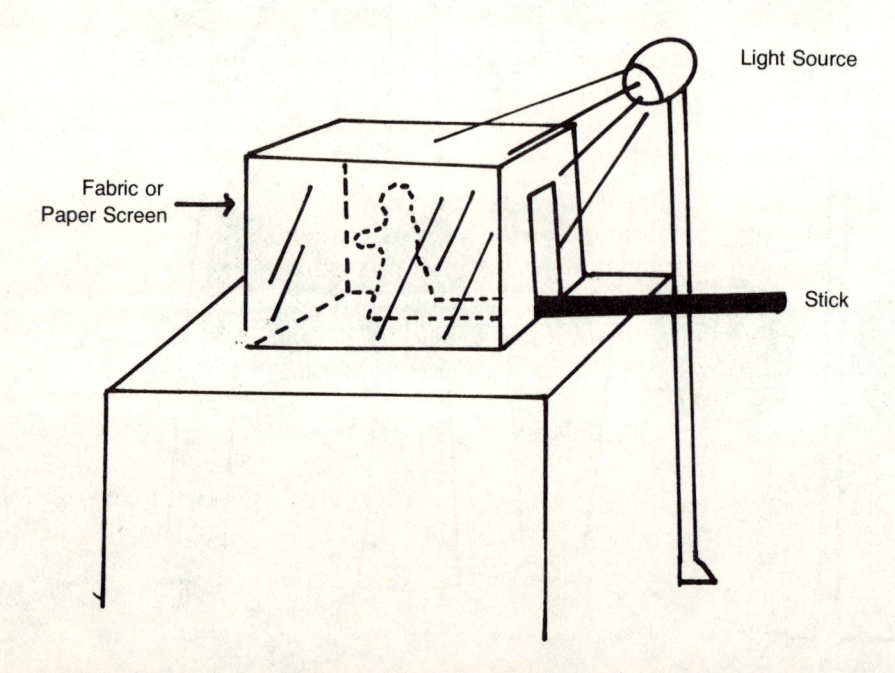

Make a Gift for the Jewish Home

In this section, you will find ideas for crafting ritual objects and other items used in the Jewish home. These gifts will add beauty and meaning to the celebration of Hanukkah, as well as to Jewish living all through the year.

MEZUZOT

A mezuzah is a little case that houses a small rolled parchment, the klaf. *Mezuzah* is the Hebrew word for "doorpost." It is based on the Biblical commandment, "And you shall write these words upon the doorposts of your house and on your gates." This verse is written by a scribe on the klaf, along with the Shema prayer and the rest of Deuteronomy 6:4–9, and 11:13–21.

The mezuzah (plural, mezuzot) is a sign indicating that a Jewish family lives in this home. Mezuzot are placed on the outside entrance and on the doorposts of each room inside, except the bathroom. A blessing is recited before attaching the mezuzot.

Shaddai, *a name for God, should be on the front of the mezuzah. This word, or its first Hebrew letter, may be seen on the back of the rolled-up parchment through a hole in the case or it may be written or carved on the case itself.*

The mezuzah should be fastened, in a slanting position, in the top third of the right-hand doorpost as you enter the room. You can use nails or thumbtacks, if the doorpost is wood, or two-sided tape or glue, if it is metal.

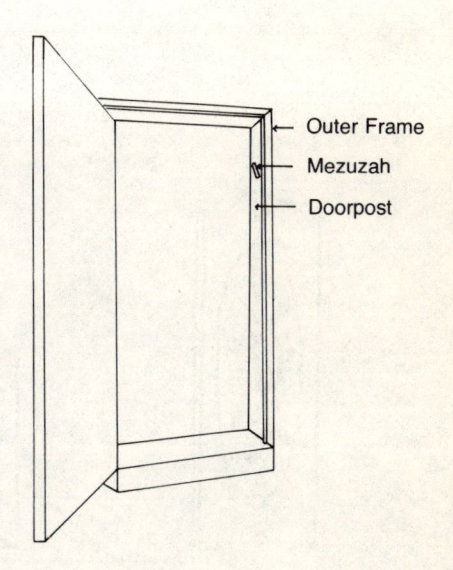

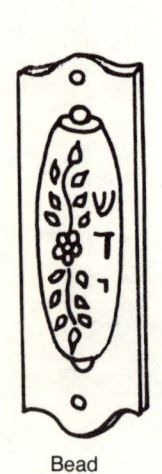

Simple Mezuzot

All of these mezuzot may be decorated with paint, felt-tip pens, or wood stain or covered with foil or colored paper. Buy a *klaf* in a Jewish bookstore or synagogue gift shop. To make a cardboard backing, use a small, shallow box or box lid or cut out a piece of cardboard. For a wood backing, cut a piece of balsa, basswood, or pine or buy a wood block in a craft store. Punch a hole at the top and bottom of the backing for hanging the mezuzah. Attach the mezuzah to the backing with craft cement.

MATCHBOX MEZUZAH

Slide open a matchbox or a box for notebook-paper reinforcements. Insert a *klaf* and close the box. Decorate the box. Attach the mezuzah to a cardboard backing.

PLASTIC PILL BOTTLE MEZUZAH

Uncap the bottle. If the bottle is clear, you may want to fill it with tiny beads or colored sand. Insert a *klaf* and replace the cap. Decorate the bottle. Attach the mezuzah to a wood backing.

BEAD MEZUZAH

Insert a *klaf* into the center hole of a long macramé bead. To secure the parchment, glue a small bead over the top and bottom openings. Paint the three beads. Glue the mezuzah to a wood backing.

SPOOL MEZUZAH

Insert a *klaf* into the center hole of an empty spool of thread. To secure the parchment, insert a small cork into the top and bottom openings. Decorate the spool. Glue the rims of the spool to a cardboard backing.

Matchbox

Plastic Pill Bottle

Bead

Spool

Instant Papier-Mâché Mezuzah

Materials:

wax paper
instant papier-mâché (from craft store)
container
water
modeling tools (knife, stick, spoon, fork)
poster or acrylic paint, any color
brush
clear plastic spray
klaf (Jewish bookstore or synagogue gift shop)

Method:

1. Cover the work surface with wax paper.
2. Mix the papier-mâché and water in the container according to package directions. Knead until it has the consistency of clay. Add more mâché if it is too wet and more water if it is too dry.
3. Mold the mâché into a shape that will fit a doorpost.
4. With the modeling tools, carve a pocket-like opening in back of the mezuzah to hold the *klaf*. You may also carve a smaller opening into the front, so the Hebrew lettering on the rolled parchment will be visible.
5. Poke a nail hole at the top and bottom of the mezuzah, so it can be hung.
6. You may use the modeling tools to carve more texture or other designs on the mezuzah. Let dry at least 24 hours. If the mâché is thick or the weather is humid, it may take longer.
7. Decorate the mezuzah with paint. Let dry.
8. For a glossy finish and protective coat, spray with clear plastic. Let dry.
9. Insert the *klaf*.

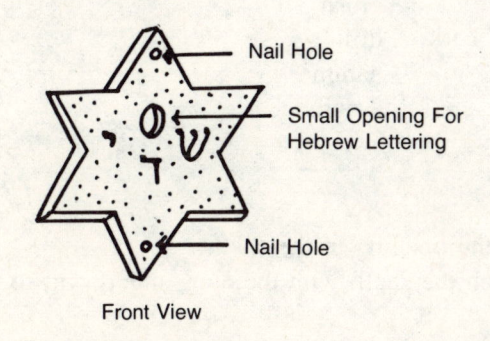

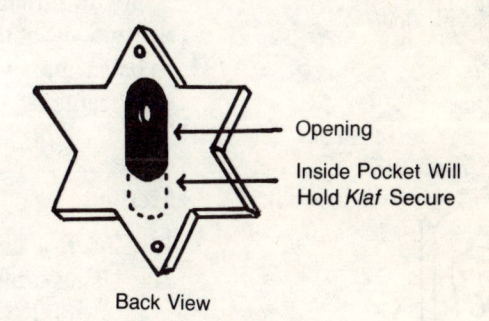

Wood Mezuzah

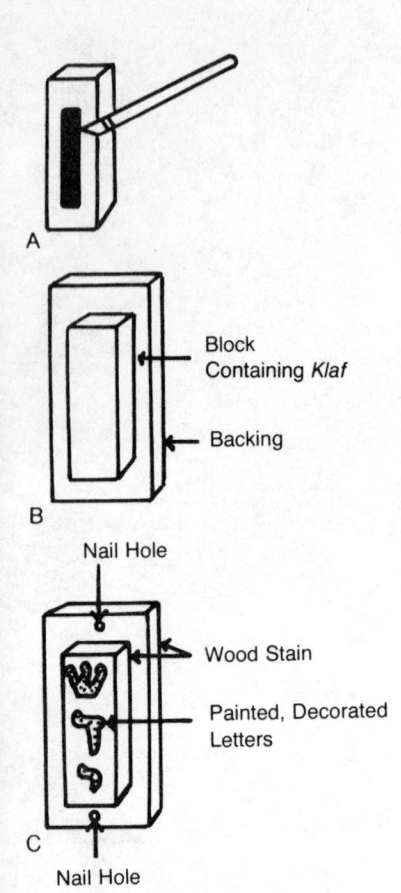

Materials:

balsa wood or basswood:
  1 piece, 2½" long × 1" wide × ½" thick
  1 piece, 3½" long × 1½" wide × ¼" thick
craft knife
klaf (from Jewish bookstore or synagogue gift shop)
wood glue
fine sandpaper
hammer
nail
wood stain, any color
brush or rag
acrylic or oil paint, any colors
fine brush

Method:

1. With the craft knife, carve an oblong opening on one side of the smaller block of wood (figure A). Insert the *klaf* in the opening.
2. Glue the block containing the *klaf* with the open side down to the larger block of wood. This backing will hold the parchment in place (figure B).
3. Sand the wood, if needed. With the hammer and nail, make a hole at the top and bottom of the backing for hanging the mezuzah.
4. Using a brush or rag, stain the wood. Let dry.
5. Decorate with paint (figure C). Let dry.

Seashell Mezuzah

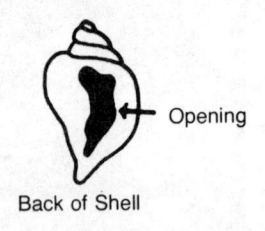

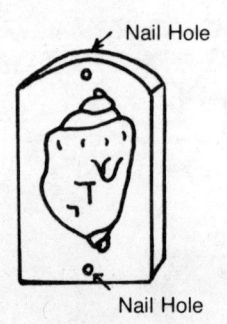

Materials:

seashell
klaf (Jewish bookstore or synagogue giftshop)
driftwood, a thick piece of bark, balsa, basswood, or pine
craft cement
wood stain or acrylic paint, any color
brush
drill
hammer
2 nails

Method:

1. Insert a parchment into the opening in the shell.
2. Using craft cement, attach the shell, with the open side down, to the wood.

3. If using balsa, basswood, or pine, stain or paint the wood. Decorate the shell with paint.
4. To hang a driftwood- or bark-backed mezuzah, drill top and bottom nail holes in the backing; hammer nails through the holes going into the doorpost. To hang a balsa-, basswood-, or pine-backed mezuzah, hammer nail holes through the wood going into the doorpost.

Clay Mezuzah

Materials:

clay that air hardens or "fires" hard in home oven
knife
nail
household aluminum foil
klaf (from Jewish bookstore or synagogue gift shop)
craft cement
acrylic paint, any color
brush

Method:

1. To make the backing, model a block of clay, as shown in figure A, about ¼" thick × 1" wide × 5" long.
2. To make an opening for the *klaf,* cut out a section of the backing, as shown in figure B.
3. To allow room for the parchment when the cutout section is replaced, make the backing thinner by cutting it in half, as shown by the dotted lines in figure C. Keep one half and save the other half for a different project.
4. To make the front of the mezuzah, form a block of clay the same thickness, width, and length as the backing. Cut it into three strips. Roll each strip into a coil.
5. Braid the coils together. Attach the braid to the backing by wrapping the top and bottom strips of braid around the backing (figure D). Gently press in place.
6. Shape the three Hebrew letters, shown in figure E, out of clay.
7. With a nail, poke a hole at the top and bottom for hanging the mezuzah (figure D).
8. Place the mezuzah case, the section saved from the back, and the letters on a sheet of foil. Bake according to package directions. If you use clay that air hardens, this step may be eliminated; leave out to harden.
9. Insert the *klaf* into the cutout section in back of the mezuzah. Secure

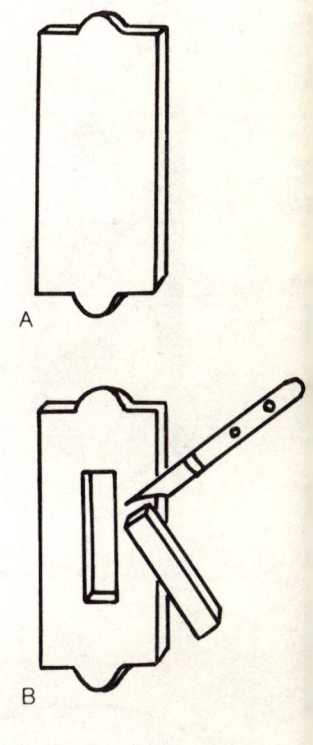

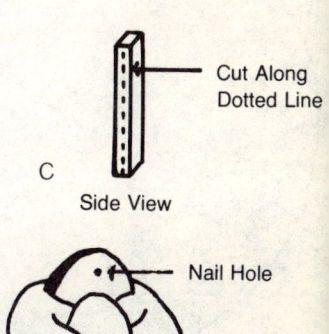

the parchment by replacing the strip you cut from the back; the tight fit holds it in place.
10. Cement the letters on the front of the mezuzah (figure F). Let dry.
11. Decorate the completed mezuzah with paint. Let dry.

KIPPOT

A kippah (plural, kippot) is a small hat or skullcap traditionally worn by men and boys. In Yiddish, it is called a yarmulke. *Some people wear a kippah all the time; others wear it only while eating or during prayer.*

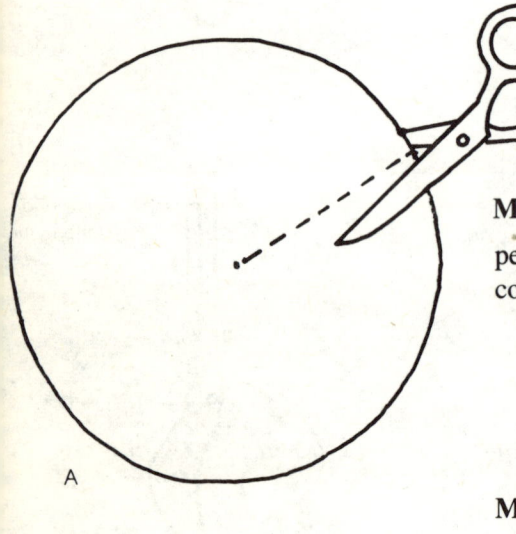

Paper Kippah

Materials:

pencil
compass (or round object about 7" in diameter)
construction paper, any color
scissors
glue or stapler

Optional: paint, brush

Method:

1. Place the pencil in the compass. Draw a circle, about 7" in diameter, on the paper. Cut out the circle.
2. Draw a dot in the center of the circle. Make a straight cut from the outside edge of the circle to the penciled dot, as shown by the dotted line in figure A.
3. Form a hat shape by overlapping one edge (figure B). Secure with glue or staples.
4. To flatten the point, hold the kippah, pointed side down, on a hard surface. Place your fingers in the hat and gently push down (figure C).
5. You may decorate the kippah with paint (figure D).

Hand-painted Kippah

Materials:

paper
pencil
dressmaker's carbon, white, if kippah is dark, dark color if kippah is light (sewing or variety store)
cellophane tape
1 store-bought kippah, any color (from Jewish bookstore or synagogue gift shop)
straight pins
tool for writing on carbon paper (ball-point pen, pointed orange stick, or sharpened pencil)
1 piece of cardboard
acrylic paint, any colors
fine brush

Method:

1. Most kippot are sewn together in four sections. On the paper with a pencil, draw a design for each section of the kippah.
2. To transfer the design, tape one of the drawings on a piece of dressmaker's carbon (it doesn't smear). Place the carbon on a section of the kippah and secure with straight pins. Trace the outline of the drawing, using one of the writing tools. Remove the pins, pattern, and carbon. Repeat for each drawing.
3. Place the piece of cardboard inside the kippah to make a firm, smooth work surface and to prevent paint from going through.
4. Fill in each design with an even coat of paint. Let dry, then remove cardboard. Clean the brush with water before storing.

Hand-sewn Kippah

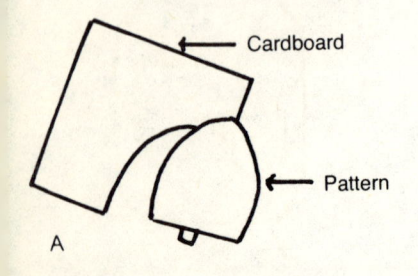

Materials:

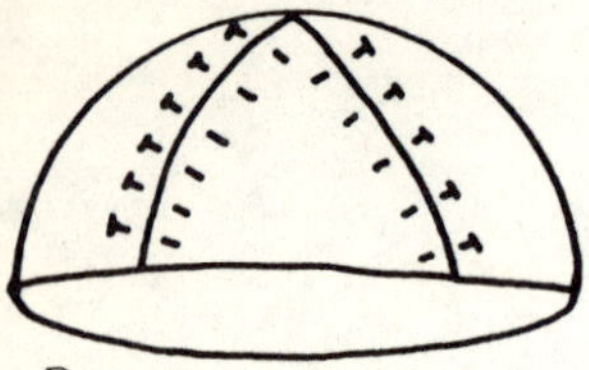

thin cardboard	straight pins	thread, same color as fabric
pencil	needle	1 piece of fabric (felt, velvet, silk,
scissors		satin, or leather), 12" square

Optional: tape, hole punch, leather lace, embroidery floss, liquid embroidery, textile or acrylic paint, scrap material

Method:

1. To make the pattern, draw the shape of one section of the kippah on cardboard (figure A). Cut it out.
2. To make one section, place the cardboard pattern on the fabric and draw around it. Four sections make up one kippah. Cut out the four sections.
3. Pin the fabric sections together (figure B). (If you use leather, tape instead of pinning).
4. To make the kippah, sew the sections together. Remove the pins. The

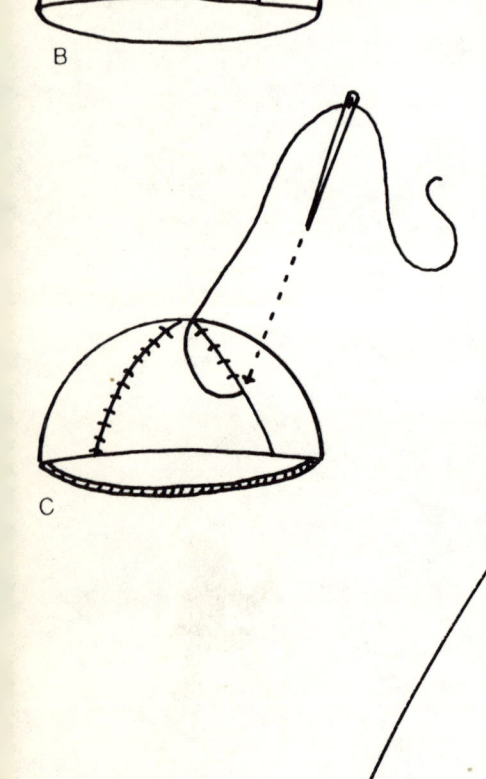

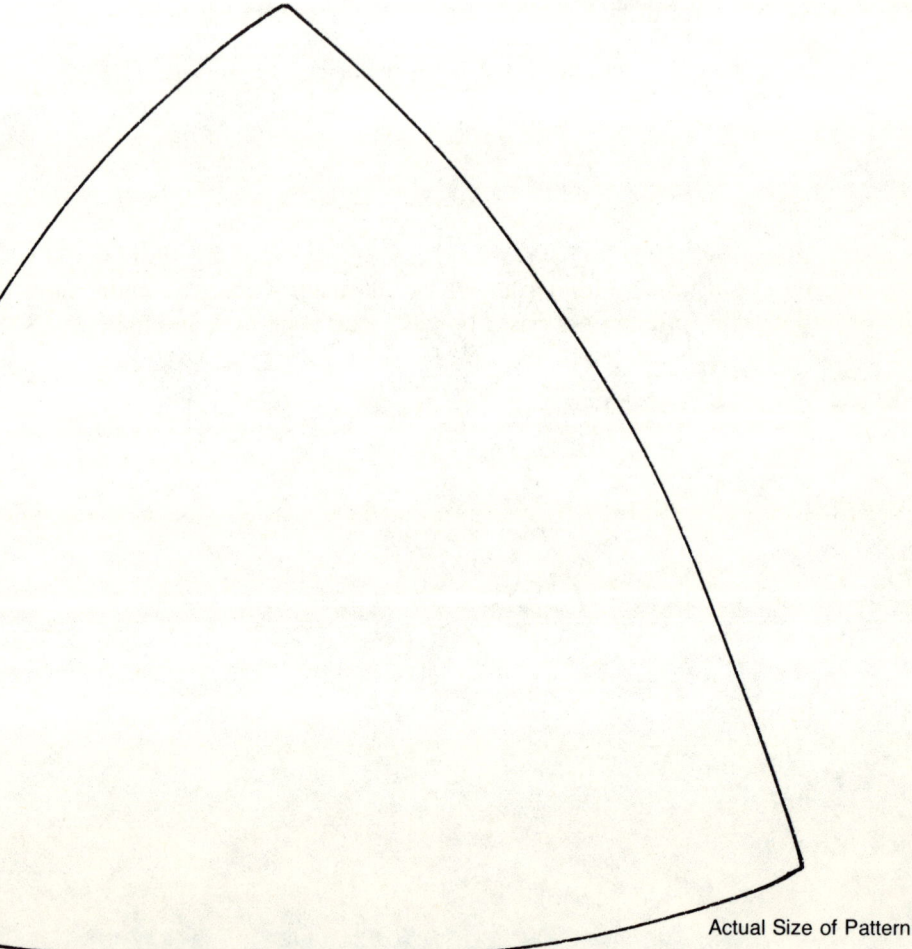

Actual Size of Pattern

bottom of the kippah may be turned under and sewn (Figure C). (If you use leather, punch evenly spaced holes around each section of the kippah. Sew with lacing. Leather does not need to be hemmed).
5. You may decorate the kippah with embroidery floss, liquid embroidery, or textile or acrylic paint. You may also sew on pieces of cutout scrap material for an appliqué design.

WINE DECANTERS

Wine plays an important role in much of Jewish life. The Kiddush (meaning "sanctification") is the prayer recited on the Sabbath and other holidays before drinking wine. During the eight days of Hanukkah, the Sabbath will occur at least once.

Make your own decanter and fill it with wine. Insert a cork top, tapered to fit the decanter.

Simple Wine Decanters

MOCK STAINED GLASS DECANTER
Start with a clear glass bottle. Draw a design on the bottle with a black permanent felt-tip pen. Fill in the drawing with permanent felt-tip pens in assorted colors.

TAPE AND SHOE-POLISH DECANTER
Start with masking tape, ¾" wide. Rip off pieces, each about ½" to ¾" long. Press them firmly to the glass, overlapping, until the entire bottle is covered. Using any color paste polish, thoroughly coat the entire tape-covered bottle, rubbing the paste in well. Buff with a clean cloth.

ACRYLIC PAINTED DECANTER
Cover the entire surface of a bottle with a base coat of gesso (from craft store). Let dry. With acrylics, paint a design and let dry. Clean the brushes with water.

Mock Stained Glass

Tape And Shoepolish

Acrylic Painted

Textured Wine Bottle

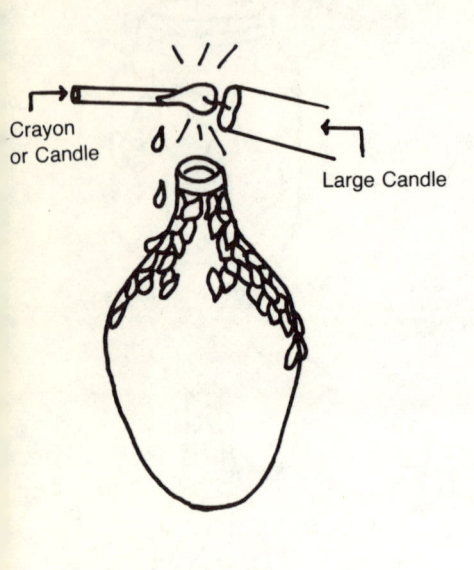

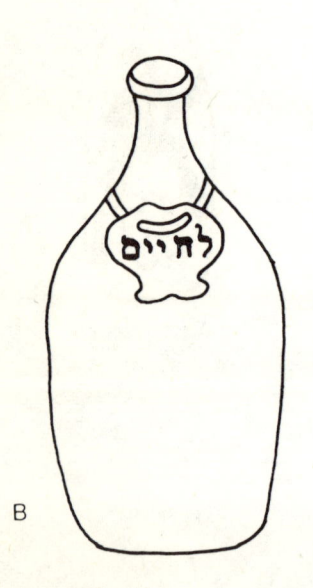

Materials:

1 large candle
1 glass bottle, any size
candle scraps or crayon scraps, assorted colors
cork tapered to fit bottle

Method:

1. Light the large candle.
2. Place the bottle on the table. To make the drippings on the bottle, take the lighted candle in one hand and a candle scrap in the other hand. Hold the candle scrap next to the flame of the lighted candle, allowing the drippings to fall on the bottle. Continue, alternating colors, with each drip slightly overlapping the next. When you have finished, none of the bottle should show through.
3. If you are using crayon scraps, peel off any paper, then follow the directions for using wax. You may have to wipe or stroke the melting crayon on the bottle.
4. To use, fill the wine bottle with wine and insert the cork top.

Label for Wine Decanter

Materials:

1 thin sheet of aluminum (from home supply center)
pencil
heavy-duty scissors
hammer
awl or heavy-duty nail
tube of liquid embroidery or enamel paint and brush, any color
thong, yarn, or colored cord

Method:

1. With the pencil, draw a design or lettering on the aluminum. Figure A shows the Hebrew toast *l'hayyim,* "to life."
2. Cut out the label.
3. Using the hammer and awl or nail, punch a hole on each side of the label.
4. Pencil a design on the label. Fill in the design with liquid embroidery or enamel paint. Let dry.
5. Thread the thong through the holes in the label and tie it around the neck of the bottle (figure B).

MIZRAHIM

Mizrah is the Hebrew word for "east." When praying, Jews always face east, toward the site of the ancient Temple in Jerusalem. The eastern wall of a room in a home or synagogue may be decorated with a wall hanging, a mizrah *(plural* mizrahim*). You can make mizrahim from any material—paper, fabric, wood—use your imagination and experiment.*

To hang the mizrah, attach a glue-on picture hanger to the back or insert in a frame. Garage sales and flea markets are a good source of old, interesting frames.

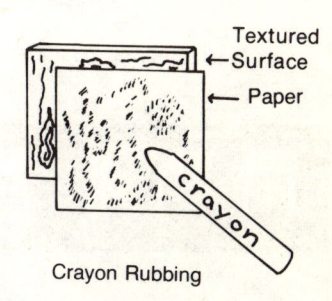

Simple Mizrahim

CRAYON-RUBBING MIZRAH

Try drawing a design on paper using only the side of a crayon. You may cut notches in the side of the crayon before drawing. Try placing the paper on a textured surface when you crayon the design. You may use different surfaces for one picture (sidewalk, tree trunk, plastic doily, wood paneling, textured tile floor).

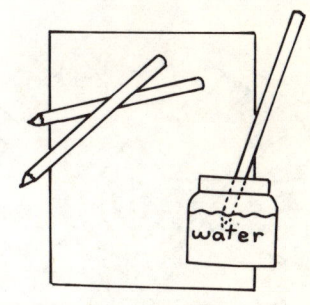

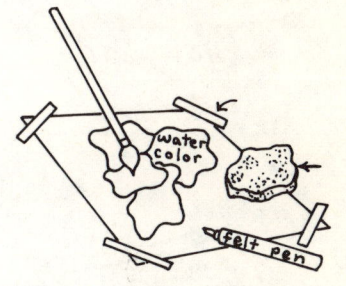

PENCIL-PAINTED MIZRAH

Dip the point of a colored pencil into water and draw while the tip is still wet. This will produce a painted look on paper or poster board.

WATERCOLOR AND PEN MIZRAH

Tape a piece of paper to the work surface. Wet the paper well and brush on watercolor paint. The colors will blend. Use felt-tip pens to add designs. The pen lines will "bleed," creating a pretty, soft effect. If the paper starts to dry while you are working, sprinkle with a little more water.

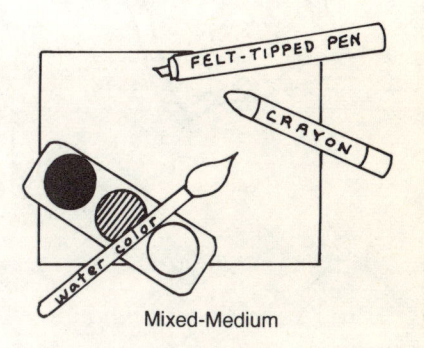

MIXED-MEDIUM MIZRAH

Draw a design on paper or heavy cardboard, using a mixture of media: watercolor background with felt-tip pen drawings or crayon drawings with pastel highlights. To prevent a pastel drawing from smearing, spray with a fixative (from craft store) and let dry.

COLLAGE MIZRAH

Draw a design on construction paper, poster board, or fabric.
Tear or cut shapes from different kinds of paper (aluminum foil, wax paper, crepe paper, colored tissue paper, construction paper, newspaper). Glue the pieces within the outline of the design.

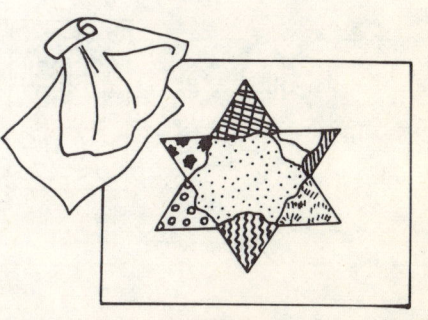

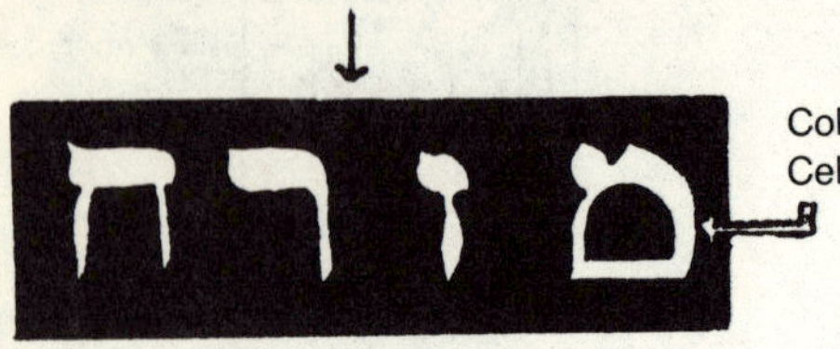

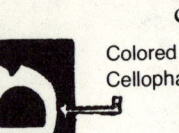

MOCK STAINED GLASS MIZRAH

Cut shapes from a sheet of black construction paper. Glue colored cellophane or colored tissue paper to the back of the paper.

BRIGHT CRAYON MIZRAH

Use fluorescent crayons to draw a design on paper, fabric, or sandpaper. To set the colors, place the picture face down on a sheet of paper and iron the back. To avoid smearing, press and lift the iron, instead of sliding it back and forth.

WINDOW MIZRAH

Place crayon shavings between two sheets of wax paper. With the iron set on low, iron the wax paper until the shavings melt together. Cut the melted picture into an interesting shape. Punch a hole at the top. Thread cord or yarn through the hole and hang in front of a window on an eastern wall.

PAPER CIRCLE MIZRAH

Draw a design on paper. With a paper punch, punch many little circles from papers of assorted colors. Glue the circles to the paper. You may pick up the circles with the point of a pin and apply a dab of glue with a toothpick. You may prefer to put glue directly on the picture, a small area at a time, or use prepasted paper that you just have to wet.

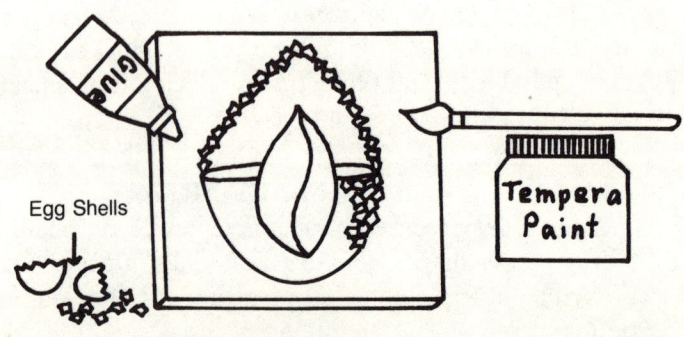

EGG-SHELL MOSAIC MIZRAH

Draw a design on paper. Glue clean, broken egg shells within the outline of the drawing. Let dry. Color the egg shells with tempera paints.

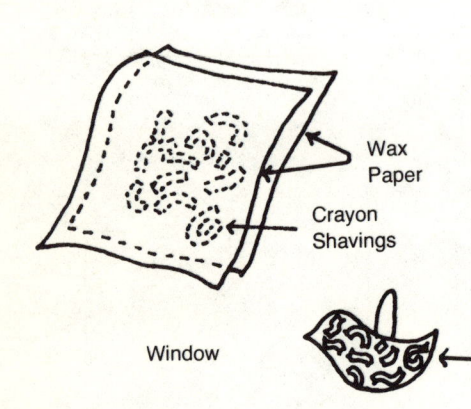

Embroidered Mizrah

Materials:

1 sheet of thin paper, 7½" × 10½"
pencil
1 piece of linen, 8½" × 11½"
dressmaker's carbon paper
straight pins
ball-point pen

embroidery floss, any colors
embroidery needle
scissors
towels
steam iron
frame, 9" × 12"

Optional: embroidery hoop

Method:

1. To make a pattern, copy on thin paper the design shown in figure A (on the next page), a design from a book or magazine, or make up your own design.
2. Place the dressmaker's carbon paper, face down, on the linen (it doesn't smear). Place the paper pattern on top and secure with the pins. Trace all the lines of the design with the pen. Remove the pins, pattern, and carbon paper. The design should appear on the linen.
3. The embroidery floss comes in six strands. To embroider the design, use only two strands at a time. You may use an embroidery hoop to keep the linen tightly stretched. You may sew with a backstitch (figure B). A split stitch (figure B) creates a more textured look.
4. Place the completed embroidery, wrong side down, on a cushion of towels. Carefully iron it, with the setting on "wool."
5. Insert the mizrah in a frame and hang on an eastern wall.

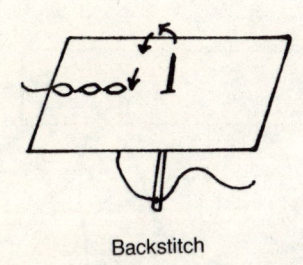

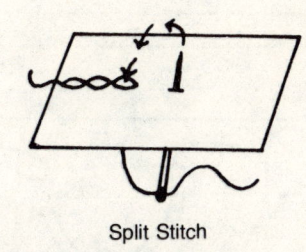

Backstitch

Split Stitch

B

92

A

Make a Gift for a...
book lover / cook / nature lover / traveler / jewelry lover / athlete / grandparent

Think about the needs, hobbies, and activities of each person for whom you want to make a gift. You can incorporate holiday symbols in some of these handcrafted originals. Each made-to-order item will be a pleasure to give and to receive.

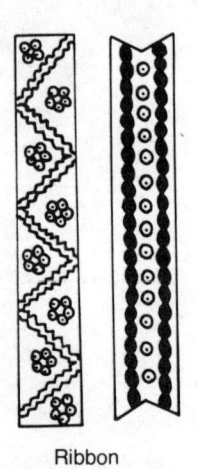

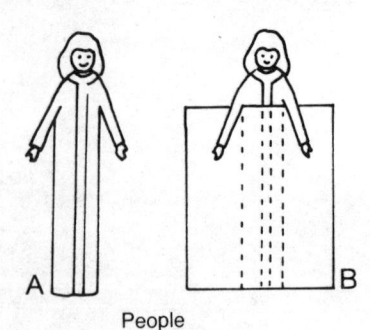

MAKE A GIFT FOR A BOOK LOVER

Bookmarks

WALLPAPER BOOKMARK
Start with a piece of cloth-backed wallpaper that has a colorful design. (Many wallpaper stores give away sample books of discontinued wallpaper.) Cut a strip, 6" long × 2" wide.

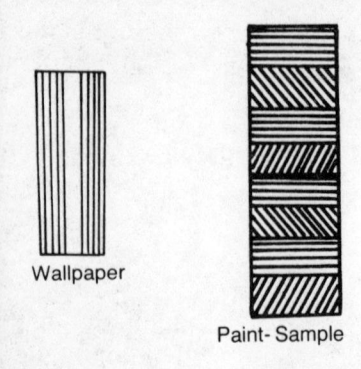

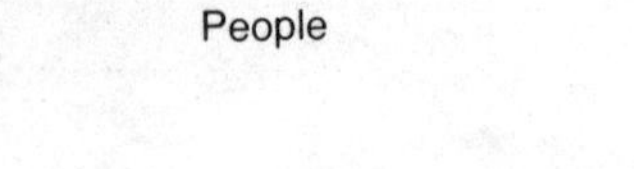

PAINT-SAMPLE BOOKMARK
Cut a strip of cardboard, 2" wide × 6½" long. Cut apart the colors from a paint-sample chart (from hardware store or home supply center). Glue each color to the cardboard.

Keep a record of books you have read by writing each new title on a different color.

COMIC STRIP BOOKMARK
Cut out part of your favorite comic strip or draw your own.

Cut two strips of clear adhesive-backed paper, ½" wider and ½" longer than the comic strip.

Peel the backing off one piece of adhesive-backed paper. Place the paper sticky side up. Center the comic strip, face down, on the sticky surface. You may back this with a second comic strip.

Peel the backing off the second piece of adhesive-backed paper. Center it, sticky side down, on the comic strip. Pressing firmly with your fingers, rub the back and front of the bookmark to help the layers stick together.

With pinking shears or scissors, slightly trim the edges of the adhesive-backed paper.

RIBBON BOOKMARK
Cut wide, brightly colored ribbon to a length of 7". Sew on rickrack or sequins.

PEOPLE BOOKMARK
Cut a strip of cardboard, 7" long × 3" wide.

Draw a human figure with arms slightly extended on the cardboard. Cut out the figure (figure A). Color the figure with crayons, paint, or felt-tip pens.

To use, place the body behind the page you want to mark, and the arms in front of it (figure B).

Bookcovers

PINPRICK BOOKCOVER

Cover a book with typing paper or colored construction paper, large enough to fold over and make flaps on both ends. Remove the paper cover and draw a design on the inside of the front cover. Using a heavy-duty needle or bulletin board pushpin, prick evenly spaced holes, close together, along the lines of the design. The holes make the design stand out when the bookcover is on the book.

FLORAL BOOKCOVER

Cover a book with plain paper, large enough to fold over and make flaps on both ends. Make an arrangement of dried flowers, leaves, or pressed butterflies (from craft store) on the front of the bookcover. To hold the arrangement in place, cover it with clear, adhesive-backed paper.

MELTED CRAYON BOOKCOVER

Start with a plain sheet of paper, large enough to cover the book, and make flaps on both ends. Place the paper on an electric warming tray which has been preheated to medium. If the paper used is thin, cover the tray with aluminum foil.

Pressing firmly with brightly colored crayons, draw a freeform design on the paper. The crayon should melt as you draw. Raise the temperature of the tray to high if the crayon has to be softened more.

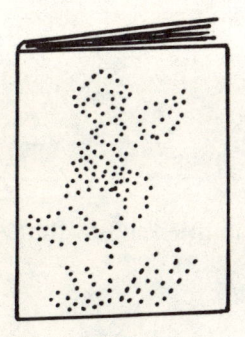

Pinprick

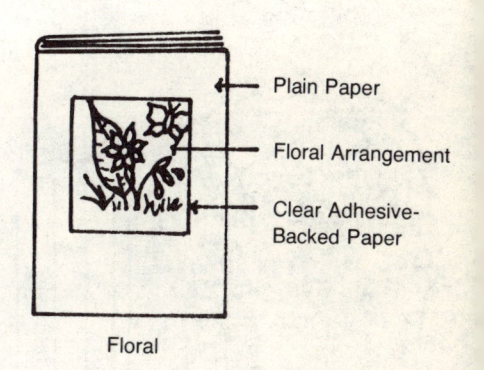

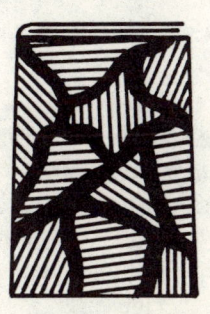

Melted Crayon

Floral

Bookplates

Materials:

plain mailing labels, any size (from stationery store)
scissors
pencil
ruler
fine or medium felt-tip pens, any color
soft art eraser (craft or art store)

Optional: small box, ribbon

Method:

1. Leave the mailing label as it is, or cut the edges into a fancier shape.
2. With the ruler, lightly draw lines and lettering on the label.
3. Trace over the penciled lines with the pens. Let dry.
4. Erase any pencil lines that still show.
5. Repeat steps 1–4 to make more bookplates.
6. You may place the labels in a box and stick one on top. Tie a ribbon around the box.

Flower Basket Bookend

Materials:

wicker basket (from craft or variety store)
small stones
artificial or dried flowers (craft store)

Optional: spray paint, any color, florist clay and dried moss (florist or craft store)

Method:

1. Leave the basket as it is or spray paint it.
2. Place stones in the basket until it is weighted down.
3. Arrange the flowers in the basket, inserting the stems in the crevices between the stones. You may use florist clay to hold the flowers in place. Cover the stones and clay with moss.
4. Repeat steps 1, 2 and 3 to make a pair of bookends.

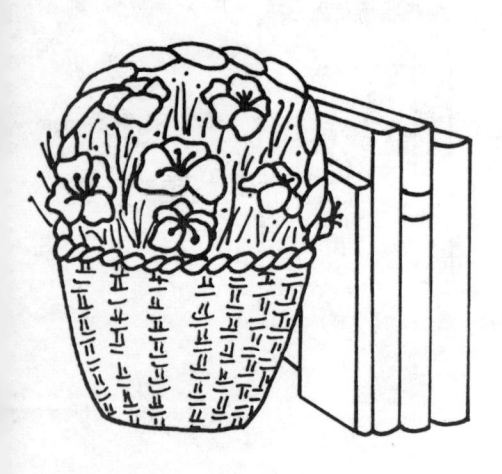

Doorknob Do-not-disturb Sign

Materials:

adhesive-backed wood-grain paper, 8″ × 12″
scissors
pencil
acrylic paint, any color
brush
heavy-duty cardboard, 4″ × 6″
hole punch
yarn, cord, or leather strip, 10″ long, any color

Method:

1. Cut the adhesive-backed paper in half.
2. Draw a design with the message "do not disturb" on one side of the paper.
3. On the second piece, draw the message "okay to enter."
4. Paint the designs. Let dry. Erase any pencil lines that still show.
5. Remove the backing from one sheet of the paper and adhere it to one side of the cardboard. Repeat with a second sheet on the reverse side of the cardboard.
6. Punch a hole at the top of the cardboard.
7. Thread yarn, cord, or a leather strip through the hole in the sign to make a loop and tie the ends. Hang the sign on a doorknob.

MAKE A GIFT FOR A COOK

"Dinner's On" Bell Pull

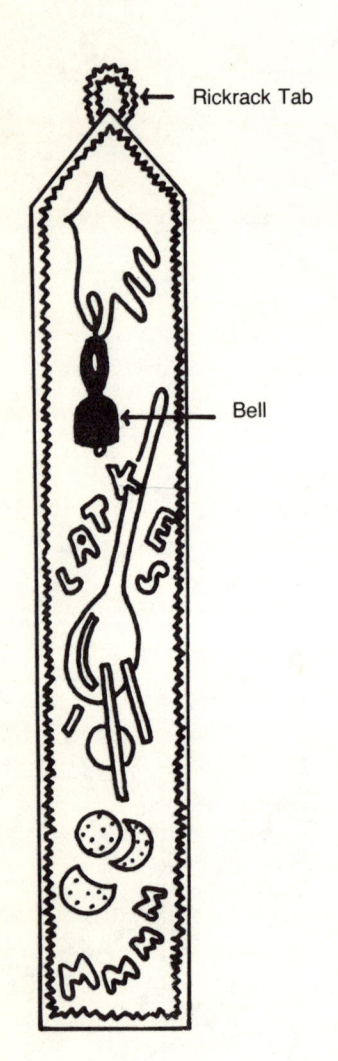

Materials:

fabric, such as felt or linen, 2' long × 6" wide, any color
scissors
rickrack, 5' × 6", any color
needle
thread
white craft cement, paste form (from craft store)
pencil
felt scraps, assorted colors
little bell (craft store)

Method:

1. To make the bell pull, cut one end of the linen or felt into a "V" shape. (If fabric such as linen is used, hem the edges to prevent fraying.)
2. Sew a rickrack tab to the point of the V.
3. Glue a rickrack border around the edges of the bell pull.
4. Draw shapes, including a hand, and letters on the felt scraps. Cut out.
5. Arrange the shapes and letters and glue onto the bell pull.
6. Sew the bell to the bell pull so it looks as though the hand is holding it.
7. Place the rickrack tab on a nail or hook on a wall. To call everyone to dinner, shake the bell pull and the bell will ring.

Magnetic "Put-ons"

Materials:

felt scraps or sponge foam sheets, assorted colors (from craft or variety store)
felt-tip pen or ball-point pen
scissors
toothpick
white craft cement, paste form (craft store)
magnetic sheet (craft store)

Optional: glitter glue, movable eyes, sequins, feathers, fabric trim

Method:

1. Draw Hanukkah symbols on felt or sponge sheets. Cut out.
2. Decorate the cutout symbols with glitter glue, different color scraps of the same fabric, or other odds and ends. Using the toothpick as an applicator, glue the decorations in place (figure A). Let dry.
3. With scissors, cut short, thin strips from the magnetic sheet. Glue them to the top and bottom (or each side) of the back of the symbol (figure B).
4. Brighten up the kitchen by attaching the symbols to the refrigerator or any other metal object.

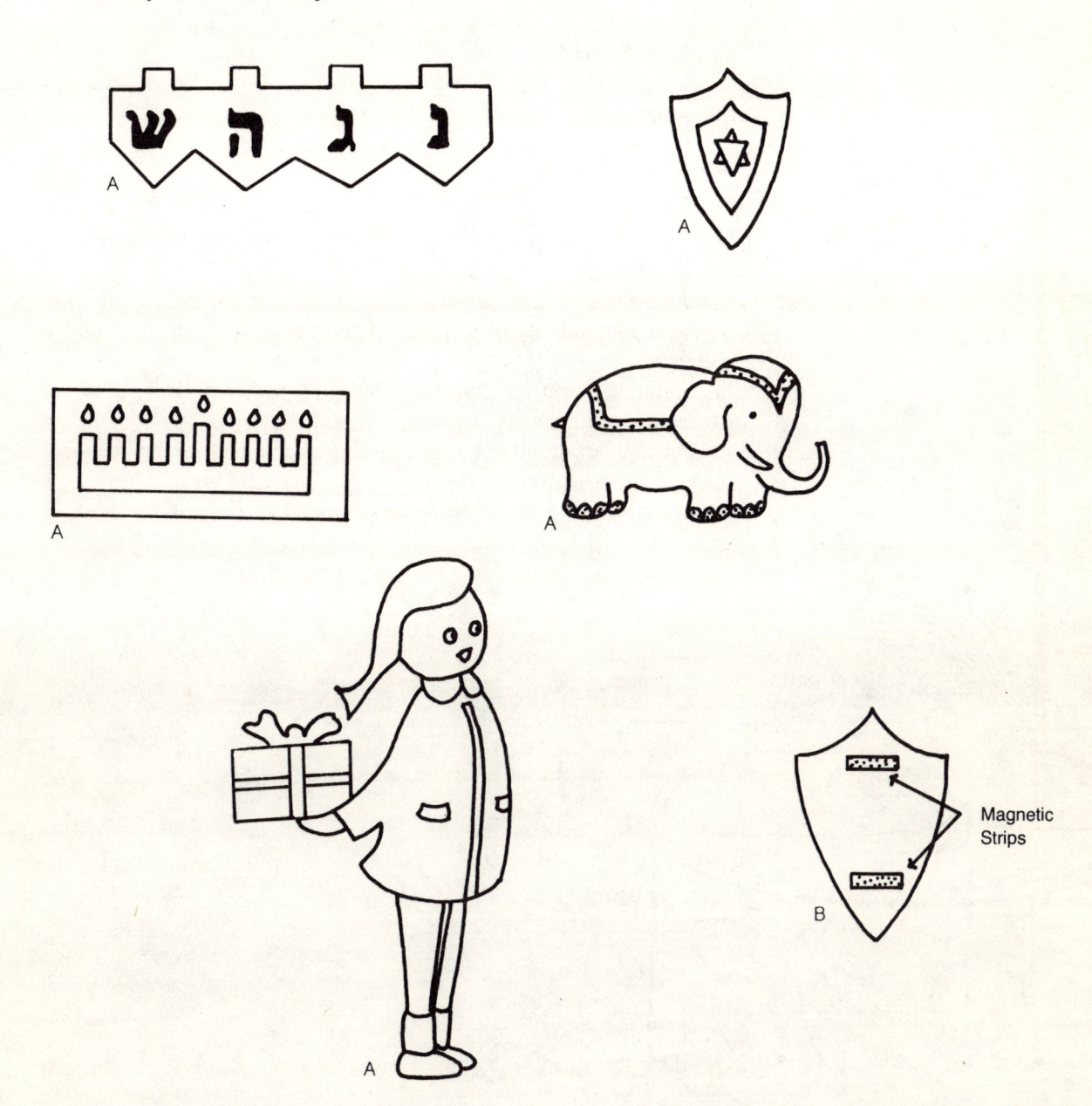

Magnetic Strips

Cookie Container

Materials:

tobacco tin or sturdy box
adhesive-backed paper or acrylic paint, any color
cardboard tube from roll of toilet tissue or paper towel
scissors
styrofoam ball (from craft store)
2 buttons
white craft cement (craft store)
curling ribbon or yarn, any color
cookies shaped like Hanukkah symbols or other Hanukkah sweets

Optional: colored paper

Method:

1. Cover the tobacco tin or sturdy box with adhesive-backed paper, or paint with acrylics. Let dry.
2. To make the neck and head, cut a section from the cardboard tube and insert it into the styrofoam ball. Glue the tube to the lid of the container.
3. Glue button eyes on the styrofoam ball. To make the hair, glue on strips of curled ribbon or pieces of yarn.
4. Symbols may be cut out of colored paper and glued on, or they may be painted on the covering paper.
5. To use, lift the lid and fill with cookies or other Hanukkah sweets.

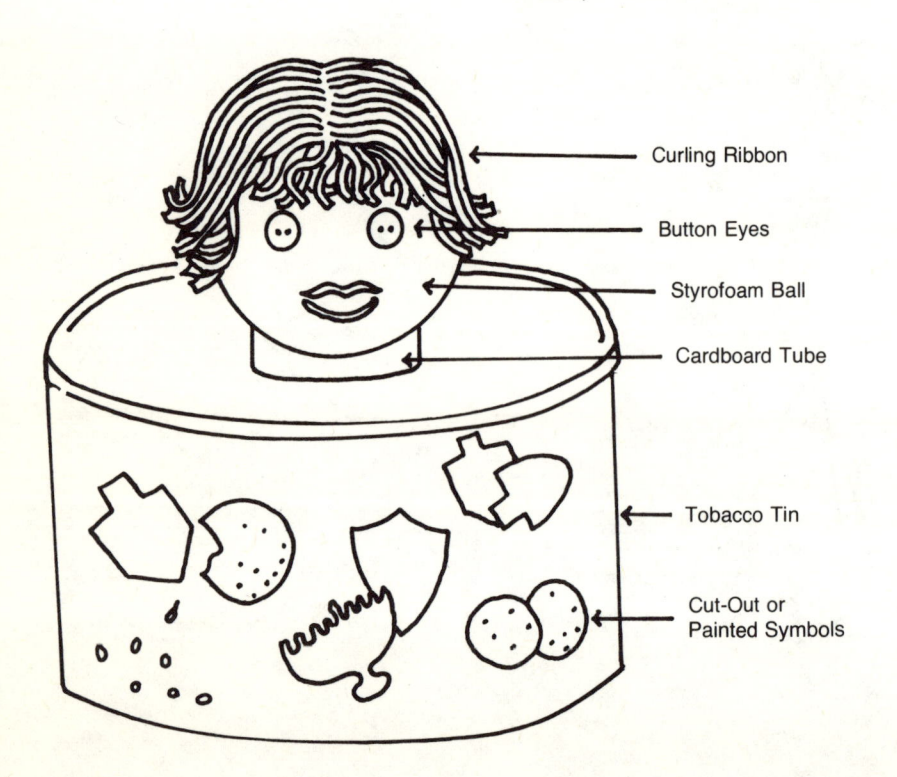

Lend-a-hand Potholder

Materials:

cotton or linen, 9" × 12", any color
pencil
scissors
straight pins
cotton batting (from sewing or variety store)
needle and thread, same color as fabric

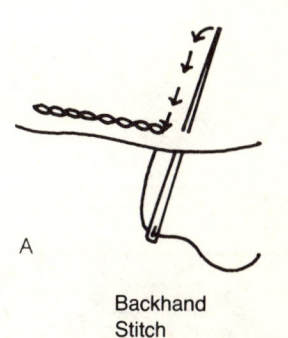

Optional: tube of liquid embroidery (craft store)

Method:

1. Keeping your fingers together, trace your left hand, then your right hand, on the fabric. Cut out the hands.
2. Place the cutout hands together, so the fingers align and the wrong side of the material faces out. Pin all around the edges of the hands except across the wrist area.
3. Using a small backhand stitch (figure A), sew all around the pinned area. Remove the pins and turn the material right side out.
4. Stuff the glove with cotton batting (figure B). Hem around the wrist area (to confine the batting) with small overhand stitches (figure C).
5. You may use the liquid embroidery to paint on a design.
6. To hang the potholder, sew on a tab of matching fabric (figure D).

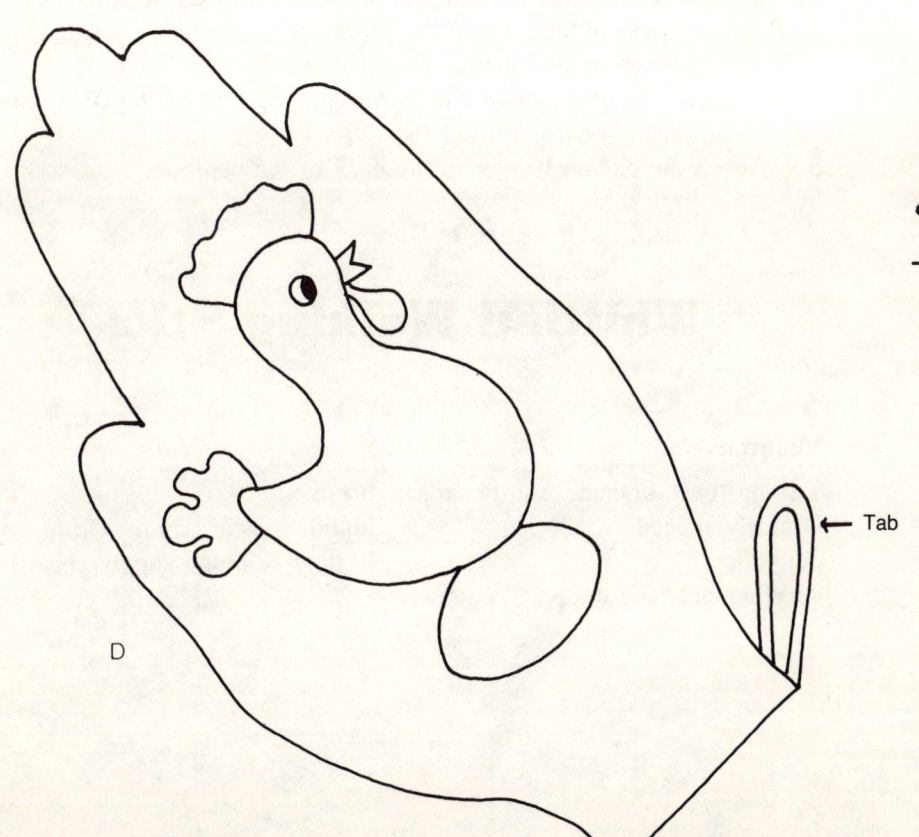

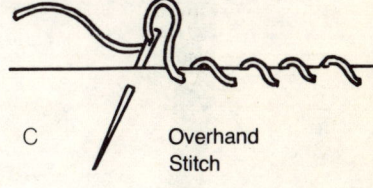

A — Backhand Stitch

B

C — Overhand Stitch

D ← Tab

MAKE A GIFT FOR A NATURE LOVER

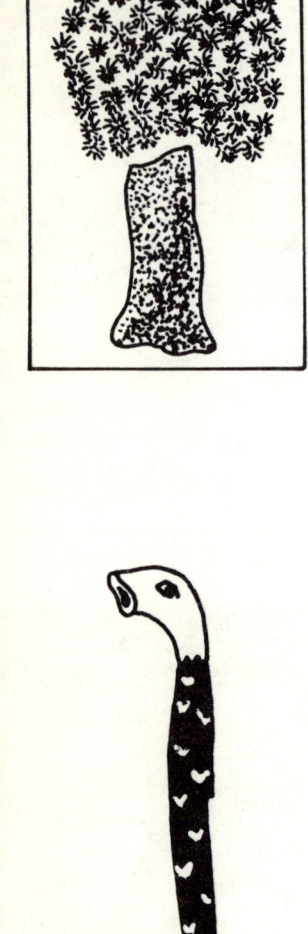

Bur Tree Picture

Materials:

pencil
sheet cork (available in rolls from craft store or lumber yard) or lightweight cardboard
craft knife
1 piece of heavy cardboard
white glue
burs (sticky balls that cover some plant seeds, such as chestnuts, available in hobby shops)
glue-on picture hanger

Optional: pieces of bark, acrylic or poster paint and brush

Method:

1. Draw the outline of a tree trunk on the sheet cork or lightweight cardboard.
2. Use the craft knife to cut out the tree trunk. Be sure to cut on a surface that will not be marred by the knife.
3. Glue the cutout tree trunk to the piece of heavy cardboard. You may glue pieces of bark within the outline of the drawing. You may paint the background of the cardboard. Let dry.
4. To make the foliage of the tree, glue burs close together on the cardboard above the trunk.
5. Attach the picture hanger to the back of the cardboard.

Whittled Walking Stick

Materials:

1 long tree branch, sturdy and nicely shaped
penknife
acrylic paint, any colors
brush
liquid plastic spray (from craft store or home supply center)

Method:

1. Whittle all or part of the bark off the branch. Keep the knife in front of the hand holding it and always whittle away from your body. You may want to whittle away bark only from selected parts of the stick.
2. Paint designs all over the stick or only on the whittled areas. Let dry.
3. When the paint is dry, spray the entire stick with liquid plastic. Let dry.

Shoe Planter

Materials:

1 old shoe—a man's old work shoe or a woman's old-fashioned high-button shoe (from thrift shop or flea market)
heavy-duty scissors
plaster of Paris
tiny potted cactus plants
heavy-duty household aluminum foil
paper towels
shoe polish, same color as the shoe

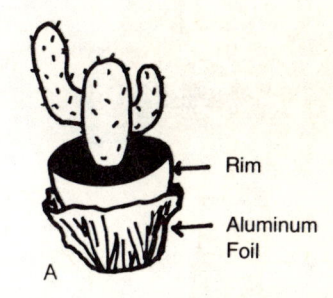

Optional: chisel

Method:

1. With the scissors, cut a hole in the top front of the toe section of the shoe.
2. Mix the plaster of Paris according to package directions. Pour it into the shoe until the shoe is nearly full.
3. Wrap a piece of foil around each potted plant, up to the rim of each pot (figure A). The foil prevents the heat generated by the plaster from cracking the pot.
4. Before the plaster hardens, insert the plants up to the rim of each pot, in the toe opening and in the top of the shoe (figure B). If the plaster hardens before you can insert the plants, just chisel out holes large enough to hold each pot.
5. Remove any foil that shows. With damp paper towels, clean any excess plaster from the shoe. Clean your hands with paper towels. Do not throw any leftover plaster down the drain.
6. Apply the shoe polish to the shoe. With paper towels, buff to a high shine.
7. The shoe planter may be used as a table decoration, doorstop, or bookend.

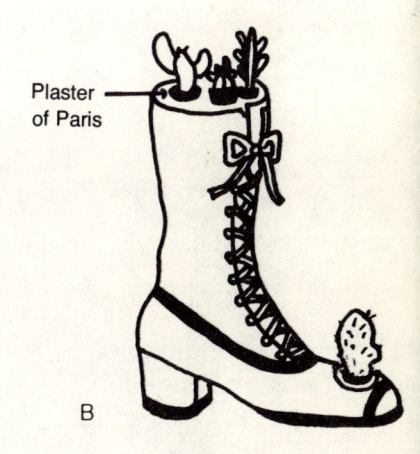

Colored Sand Planter

Materials:

colored sand, homemade (see directions below) or bought in craft store—white, green, red, light brown, yellow, blue, and black (each in a separate container)
clear glass or plastic container
long-handled spoon
thin tool (knitting needle or clear plastic wrap
potting soil for cactus or other succulent plant
small cactus or other succulent plant
box and gift wrap

Method:

To make the colored sand:
1. Place a small amount of tempera paint or food coloring in a clear container that has a cover.
2. Add clean sand from the beach or play sand for sandboxes (from home supply store), a little at a time, and shake until you get the color you want.
3. Spread the colored sand on a cookie sheet or tray covered with aluminum foil. Repeat this process using the remaining six colors. Dry the sand in the oven, set on low temperature.
4. Spoon each of the seven colors into separate containers.

To make the planter:
1. Spoon a thin layer of white sand into the clear glass or plastic container (figure A).
2. On top of the white sand, spoon three little piles of green sand, evenly spaced around the sides of the container (figure B).
3. Add a thin layer of white sand over the entire surface (figure C).
4. Rest the pointed tip of the thin tool against the side of the container and poke it (at uneven intervals) through the white sand, going deeply into the green sand. Tilt the tool back toward the middle of the container and carefully slide it out. Do this to each of the green areas. This makes an aerial view of three groups of trees (figure D).
5. To form mountains, spoon in a wavy layer of white sand, peaking it higher in some spots than others (figure E).
6. In some of the hollows or low spots in the mountains, spoon some more green sand and repeat Step 4 (figure F).
7. Mix some red, light brown, and yellow sand together and fill in the middle of the container if a hollow has formed there, building it up over the white mountains, to form new mountains (figure G).

8. Add a layer of blue sand for the sky. To form clouds, make low, but wide, mounds of white sand against the sides of the container, between layers of blue (figure H).
9. To make a bird, put a little black sand on the tip of the spoon and mound it against the side of the container. Gently slide the tool down into, and a little through, the center of the black mound. Carefully tilt the tool back toward the middle of the jar and slide it out. The bird will look as if it is flying (figure I).
10. Add another layer of blue sky, leaving a two-inch empty space at the top of the container for the cactus to be planted.
11. Place a piece of clear plastic wrap on top of the finished design.
12. Add a layer of potting soil to within one inch of the top of the container and plant a cactus or other hardy plant that needs little watering (figure J).
13. Carefully place in a box and gift wrap. Label the package "HANDLE WITH CARE," "THIS SIDE UP."

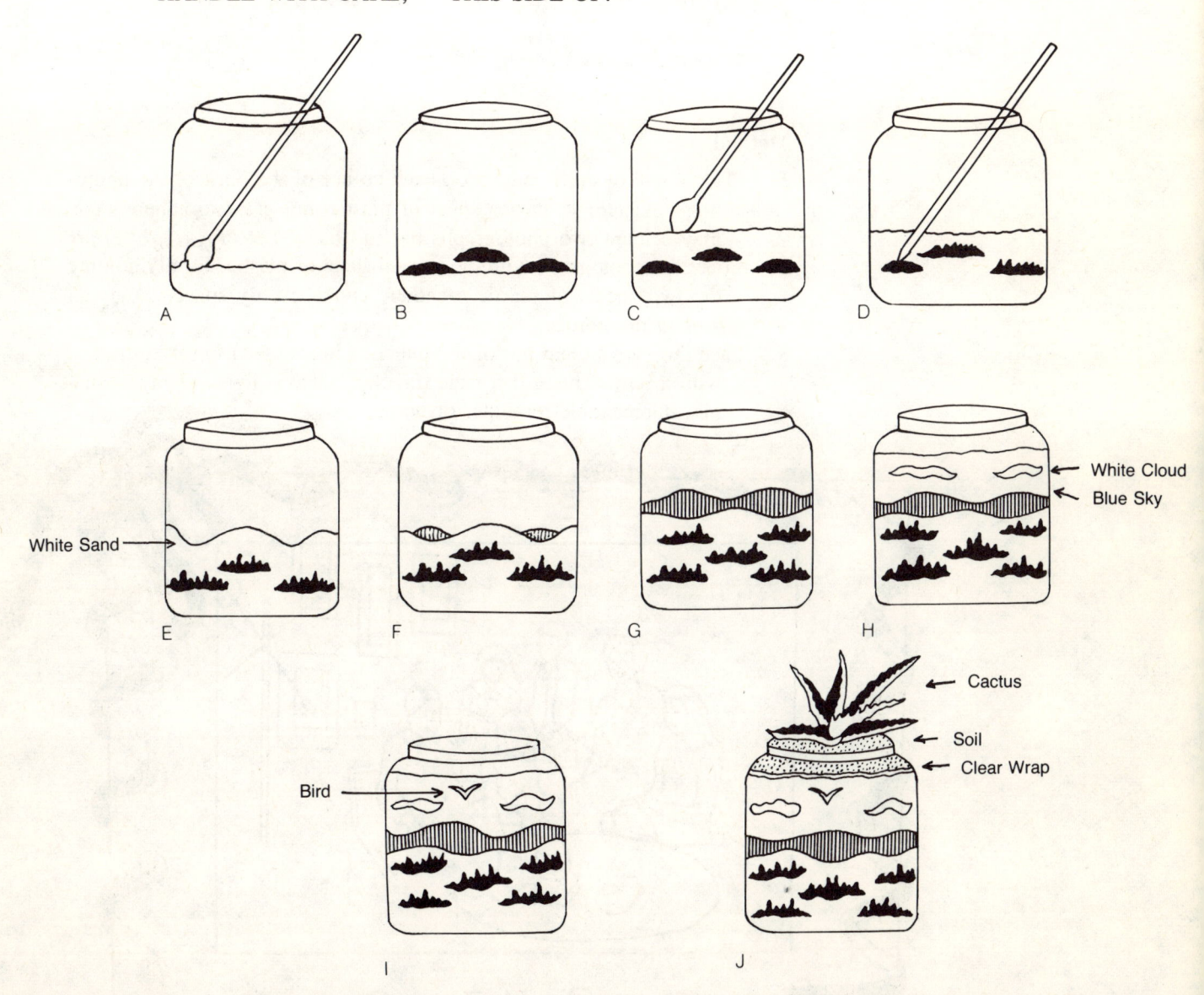

MAKE A GIFT FOR A TRAVELER

Photo in Plastic

Materials:

1 family photograph
2 sheets of plastic, 2″ longer and 2″ wider than the photo (from craft, hobby, or art store)
white craft cement, paste type that dries clear (craft store)
hole punch
yarn, any color

Optional: second photograph

Method:

1. Place a dab of craft cement on each corner of the back of the photograph. Center it on one sheet of plastic and press to adhere. You may cement two photographs back to back. Let dry.
2. Cover the photograph with the second sheet of plastic. Firmly holding the two sheets of plastic together, punch evenly spaced holes all around the border.
3. Lace the yarn in and out of the punched holes, securing it at the end with a bow. This gift for the traveler makes a lightweight, washable, unbreakable reminder of home.

Shrinking Plastic Key Holder

Materials:

plastic lid from liver container (from supermarket or butcher) or plastic that shrinks (craft store)
scissors
pencil
paper
permanent felt-tip pens, black and assorted colors
hole punch
household aluminum foil
metal key chain (craft store)

Method:

1. Carefully cut off the rim of the lid.
2. Place the rimless lid on the paper and draw around the outline. If you use a plastic sheet, draw your own outline.
3. With the pencil, sketch a design within the outline.
4. Place the plastic on top of the design. Use the black felt-tip pen to trace over the lines of the design.
5. Turn the plastic over. With the colored felt-tip pens, fill in the design.
6. Punch a hole near the top of the plastic.
7. Place the plastic, colored side down, on the foil. Put in a preheated 400 degree oven for a few seconds, or until the edges of the plastic curl, then the plastic shrinks, and the edges uncurl. Remove from the oven and let cool.
8. Remove the plastic from the foil and thread the key chain through the hole in the plastic.

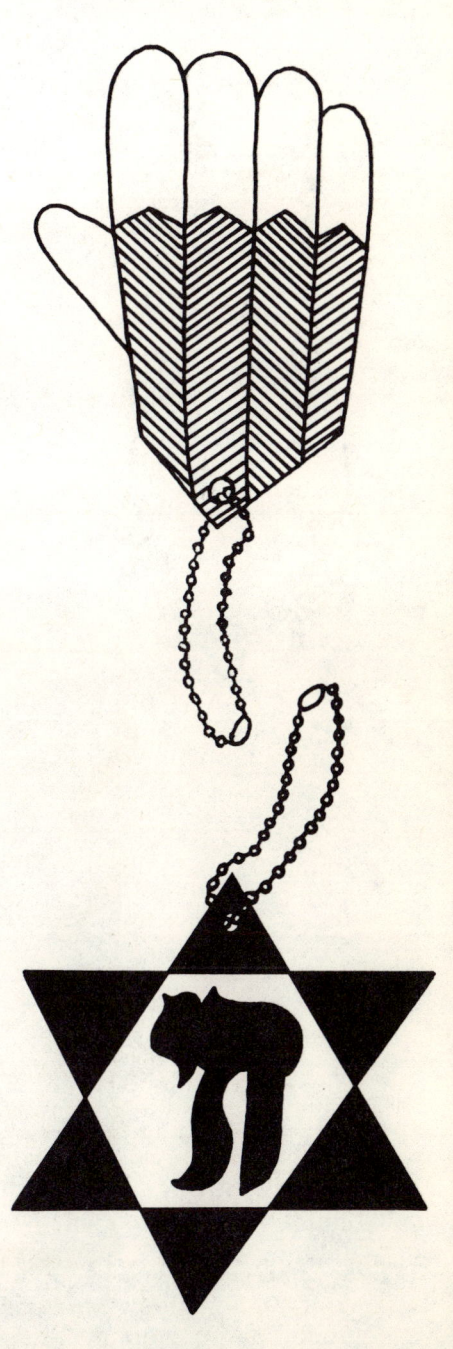

MAKE A GIFT FOR A JEWELRY LOVER

Nut Jewelry

Collect nuts or acorns from an area with trees or buy them in a supermarket. Make the nuts into jewelry to wear or to give as gifts or party favors.

PINS

Hold an acorn, filbert, or hazelnut with the pointed side down and the stem up. Glue on movable eyes (from craft store).

Paint on hair and facial features with acrylic paints and a fine brush. When the hair is dry, paint a kippah on the top of the head. Glue on a cotton beard (figure A).

With craft cement, attach a pin backing (variety, sewing, or craft store) to the back (figure B).

NECKLACE

Drill a hole through several nuts. Paint a design on each nut with acrylic paints and a fine brush. Let dry.

String the nuts on fishing line (from sporting goods store), leaving enough string so the necklace can easily slip over your head. You may use elastic thread instead of fishing line to give the necklace more stretch.

Coat the nuts with a protective finish of clear plastic spray (paint or craft store).

Craft-plaster Necklace

Materials:

newspapers
powdered craft plaster (from craft store)
disposable container
wax paper
tablespoon
paper towels

sharp instrument (nail file, nail, skewer)
liquid shoe polish, any color
rags
clear plastic spray (craft store)
jump ring (craft store)
plastic lace, leather thong, or strong yarn, any color

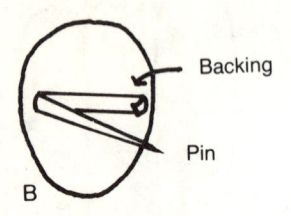

Method:

1. Cover the work surface with newspapers. Mix about one cup of plaster in the container, according to package directions.
2. Before the mixture starts to set, use the tablespoon to drop globs onto a sheet of wax paper (figure A). Do not pour leftover plaster down the drain. Clean your hands with wet paper towels.
3. Before the globs harden completely, use the sharp instrument to bore a hole through each plaster pendant.
4. When dry, use the sharp instrument to carve a design deeply into each plaster pendant (figure B).
5. Pour the shoe polish on a rag. Apply to each pendant and wipe most of it off with another rag. The polish will color the surface but not seep into the carved design. Lightly buff the etched pendant with a clean rag.
6. Coat the pendant, front and back, with plastic spray, according to directions on the can.
7. Insert a jump ring through the hole in the pendant. Thread a lace, thong, or yarn through the jump ring (figure C).

Jewelry Boxes

Egg Carton Jewelry Box

Glue macaroni in various shapes to the top of a cardboard or styrofoam egg carton (Figure A). Spray with paint suitable for styrofoam (from craft store). Let dry. To use, fill each inside indentation with jewelry (figure B).

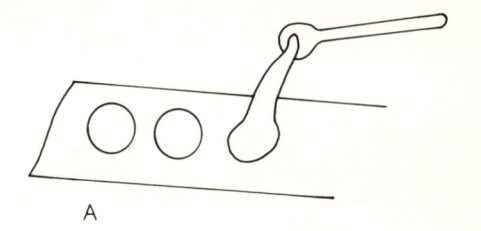

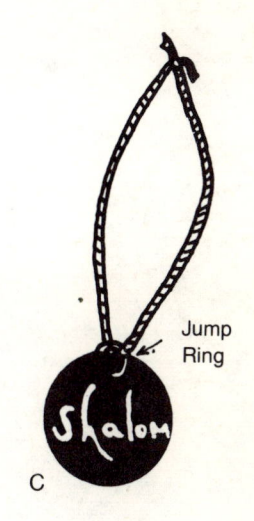

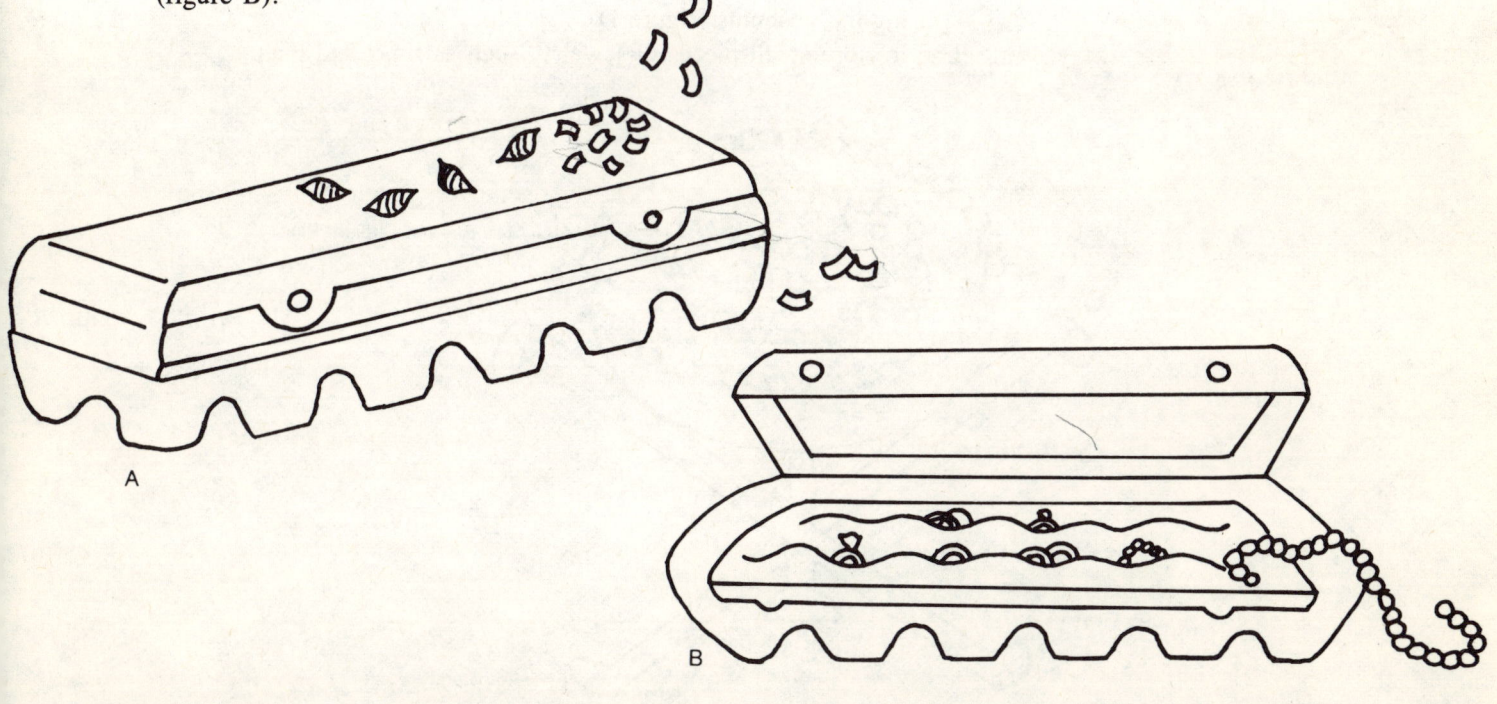

Styrofoam-egg Jewelry Box

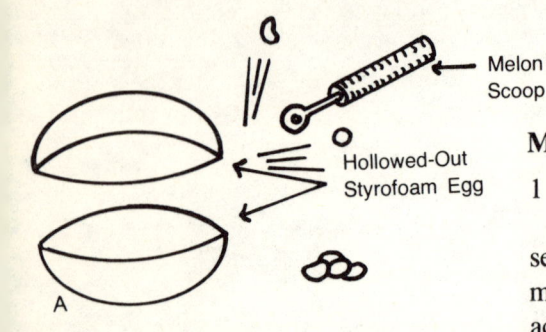

Materials:

1 large styrofoam egg (from craft store)
serrated knife or craft knife
melon scoop or grapefruit knife
acrylic polymer modeling paste (craft store)
household aluminum foil, shaped into a shallow pan
poster paint, any color
brush
straight pins or ½" sequin pins (sewing or variety store)
beads with holes smaller than the head of the pins
4 bulletin board pushpins

Optional: stand for the styrofoam egg (craft store)

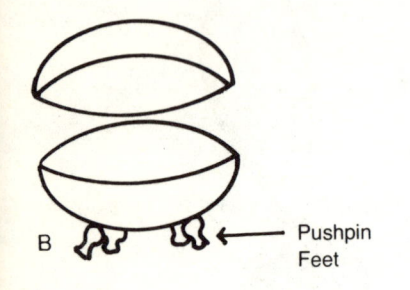

Method:

1. Cut the styrofoam in half lengthwise. Scoop out both halves of the egg with the melon scoop (figure A). Leave the walls thick enough so the beaded pins do not protrude.
2. Place a large glob of modeling paste in the foil pan. Add poster paint and mix until you have the color you like.
3. With the brush, generously coat the outside of both halves of the egg. Let dry. Coat the inside. Let dry.
4. Stick straight pins through beads (figure B). Push the beaded pins into the top (cover) of the egg in a design.
5. To make the footed stand, insert the four pushpins into the bottom half of the egg (figure C). You may place the egg on a stand instead of using the pushpins (figure D).
6. Use to store small pieces of jewelry, such as rings and pins.

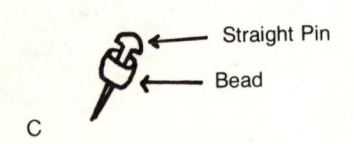

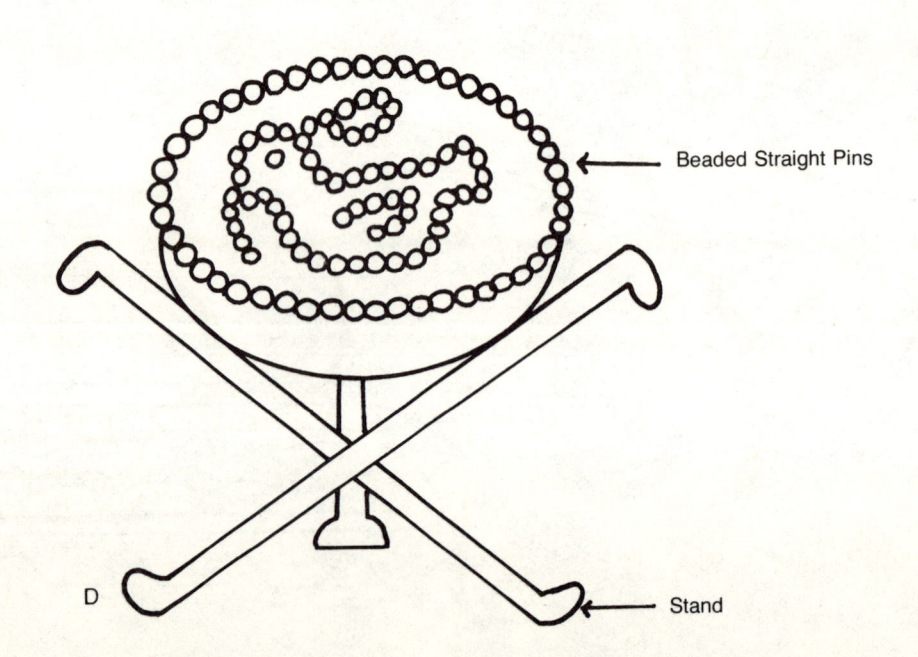

Hand Jewelry Holder

Materials:

paper
pencil
1 length of flexible wire, about 42" long (from hardware store)
wire cutter (hardware store)
acrylic paint, any color
brush
1 thick block of cork (or glue several thicknesses together) or styrofoam (craft store or home supply center)

Optional: colored stones, craft cement (craft store)

Method:

1. Draw the shape of your hand on the paper.
2. Form the wire around the drawn shape and twist the ends to hold (figure A). Trim any excess with the wire cutter.
3. Paint a design or message on the cork. Let dry. Clean the brush with water before storing.
4. Insert the twisted end of the wire hand into the cork base.
5. You may glue colored stones around the rim of the base.
6. To use, place rings on the wire fingers (figure B). Additional jewelry may be placed on the base.

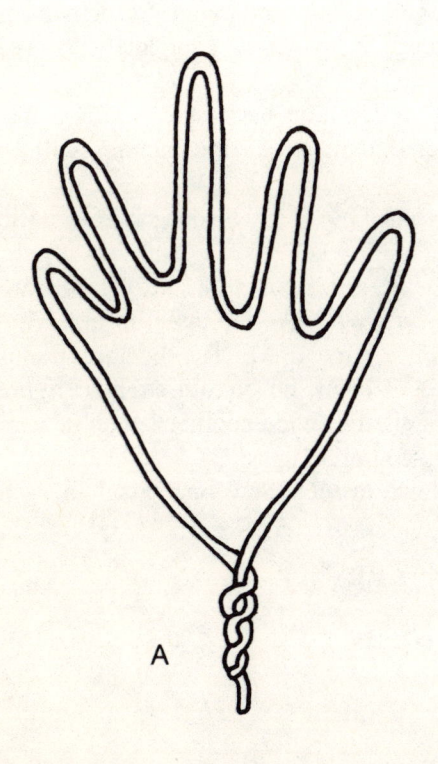

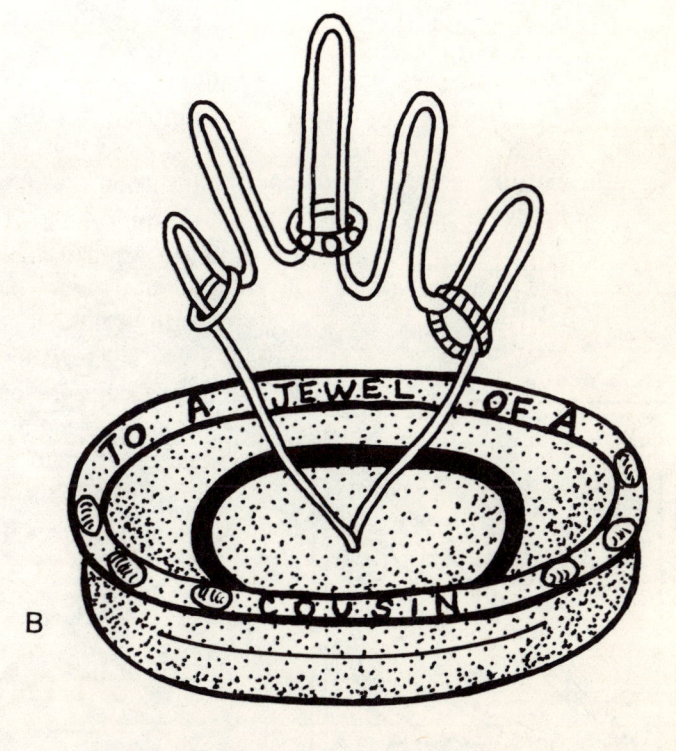

A

B

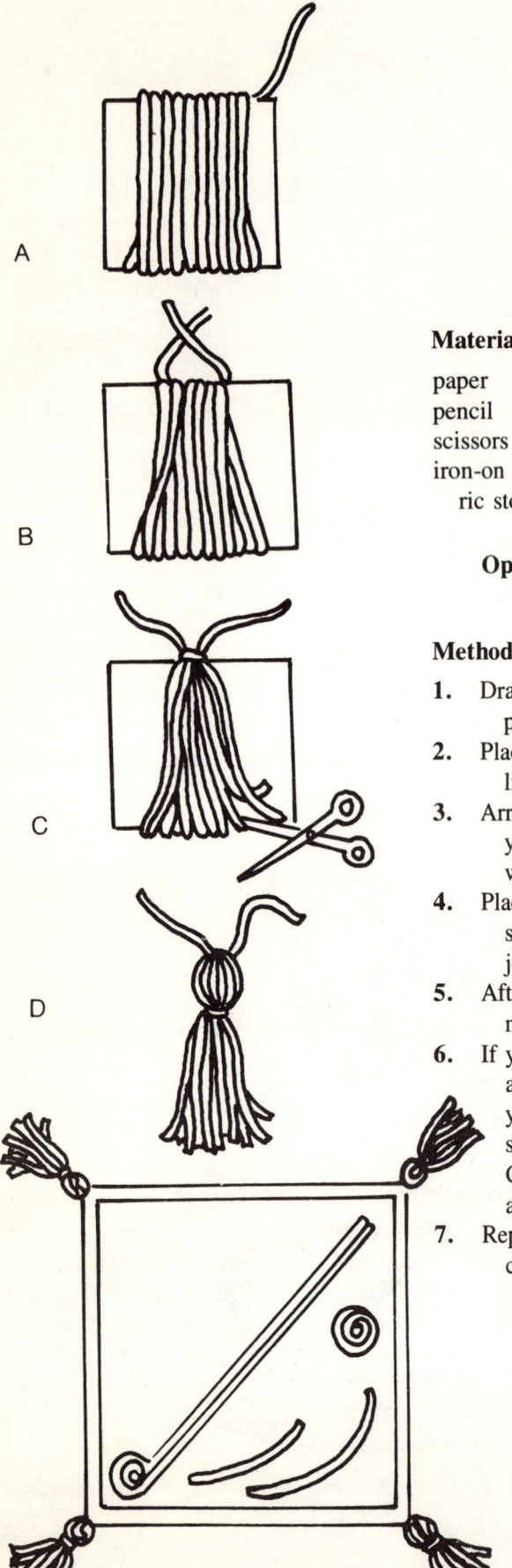

MAKE A GIFT FOR AN ATHLETE

Sweat Towel

Materials:

paper
pencil
scissors
iron-on fusible material (from fabric store)

hand towel
yarn, any color
iron

Optional: cardboard, needle, thread, same color as yarn

Method:

1. Draw a sport symbol on paper to fit on the hand towel. Cut out each part of the symbol.
2. Place the paper pattern on the fusible material. Trace around the outlines and cut out.
3. Arrange the fusible material symbols on the hand towel. Cut lengths of yarn and place on the symbol until the symbol is completely covered with yarn.
4. Place a steam iron, at "wool" setting, on each symbol for a few seconds. As the fusible material melts, the yarn pictures will be joined to the towel.
5. After using, the towel can be washed by hand, or on gentle cycle in machine, in cold water.
6. If you want to make a corner tassel, cut a piece of sturdy cardboard about 3" long, or as long as you would like the tassel to be. Wind yarn around it at least 20 times (figure A). Tie the top strands securely together (figure B). Cut apart the bottom strands (figure C). About one-half inch below the tie, wind another length of yarn around all the strands and tie securely (figure D).
7. Repeat step 6 to make three more tassels. Sew one tassel to each corner of the towel.

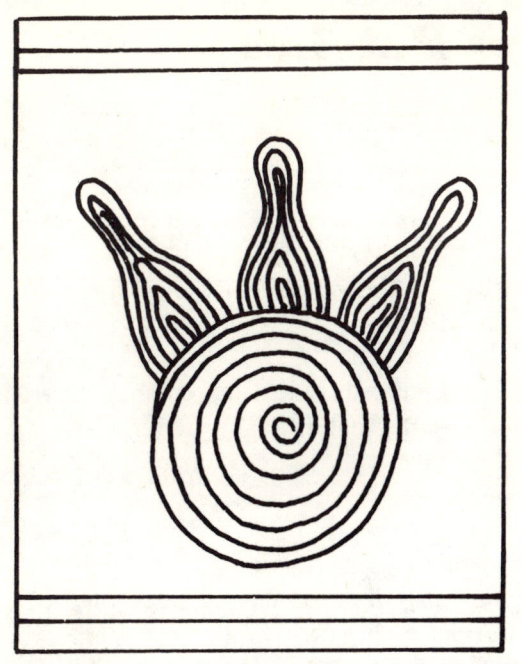

113

Bowling

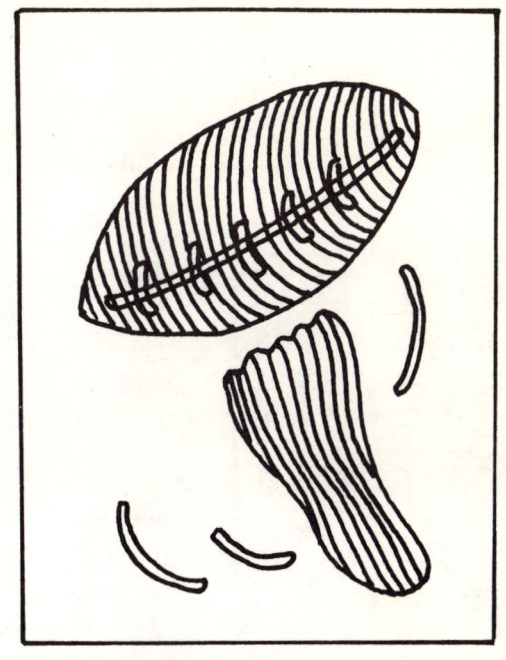

Football

Tennis

Baseball

Sports Patches

Materials:

paper
pencil
small, sharp scissors (manicure)

iron-on tape, assorted colors, about 3½" × 5"
garment (shirt, jacket, scarf)
iron

Optional: fabric, patch size, needle, thread, same color as fabric, permanent felt-tip pens, assorted colors

Method:

1. Draw a sports figure or symbol on paper (figure A).
2. Make a pattern by drawing each part of the design separately on paper, as shown in figure B. Cut out each part.
3. Place each part of the pattern on the iron-on tape, trace around it, and cut out.
4. Decide where you want to place the patch on the garment. Apply the bottom layer first, pressing with a warm iron, according to the directions on the tape package. Continue applying each section until the patch is complete (figure C).
   The tape may be applied to fabric to create a patch. The patch may then be sewn on the garment of your choice.
5. Felt-tip pens may be used to add detail to the patch design, if you wish.

More Symbols
for Sports Patches

115

Soccer

Basketball

Boxing

Baseball

Baseball

Baseball

Tennis

Jogging

MAKE A GIFT FOR A GRANDPARENT

Bulletin Board

Materials:

paper
pencil
sheet of cork, any size, or store-bought bulletin board
acrylic paint, any color
fine brush
wider brush
glue-on picture hanger
bulletin board pushpins
wrapping paper and ribbon

Method:

1. Sketch a design on paper.
2. Redraw the design on the cork.
3. Paint the design, using the fine brush for details and the wider brush for larger areas. Let dry.
4. Attach the picture hanger to the back.
5. Gift wrap the bulletin board with the pushpins.

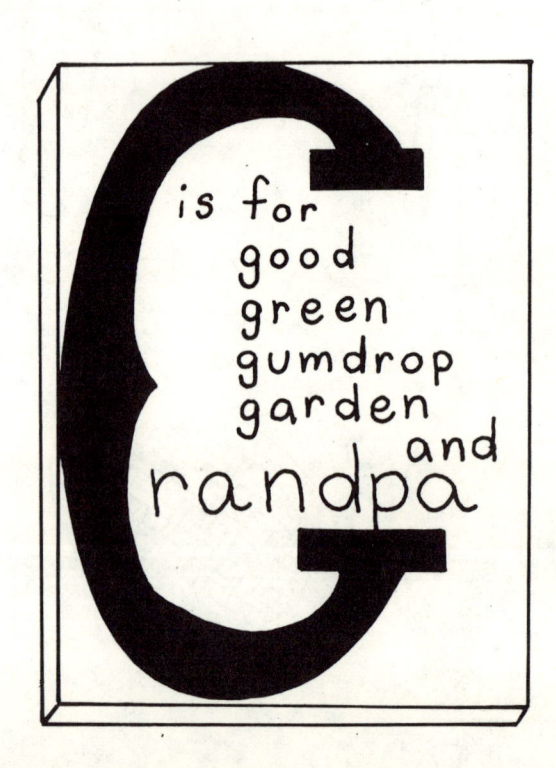

Handpainted Soap

Materials:

bars of store-bought soap
acrylic paint, any color
2 small brushes
wax (small cakes for canning, available in food stores, or a white candle, or wax from craft store)
double boiler (see step 4)
box and gift wrap

Method:

1. Decorate the top of the soap with the acrylic paint. Let dry.
2. Melt the wax over low heat in the double boiler.
3. Brush a layer of wax only over the painting on top of the soap. (Keep this brush for applying wax as it will no longer be usable for painting.) Let the wax dry hard before using.
4. NOTE: a thin layer of wax will remain in the double boiler. Use the double boiler only for crafts projects, not for food.
5. Gift wrap the soap and enclose a note to let the recipient know that a protective coating of wax will allow the soap to be used without washing away the design.

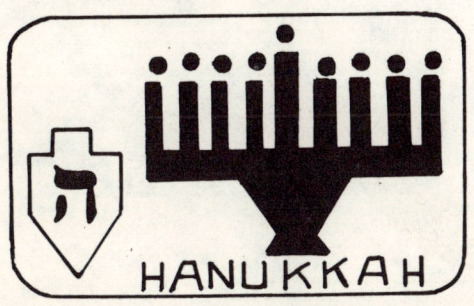

Basket Pincushion

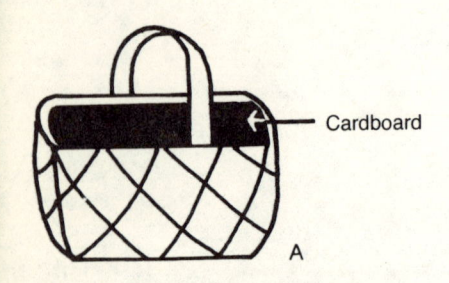

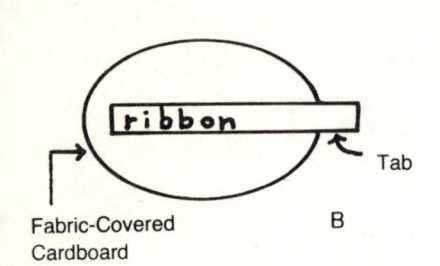

Materials:

small basket or other container (with handle, if available)
1 piece of lightweight cardboard
scissors
cotton
white glue
fabric
ribbon
straight pins

Method:

1. Cut the cardboard to fit snugly inside the top of the basket (figure A).
2. Remove the cardboard. Glue a mound of cotton all over one side of the cardboard.
3. To make the pincushion, wrap fabric around the cotton-covered cardboard. Glue the fabric to the back. Let dry.
4. Cut ribbon to go across the bottom of the cardboard and extend to form a tab (figure B).
5. Glue ribbon around the top rim of the basket and to the handle, if it has one.
6. Stick pins in the pincushion. Place extra pins inside the container. Cover the container with the pincushion (figure C). Use the tab to lift up the pincushion when extra pins are needed.

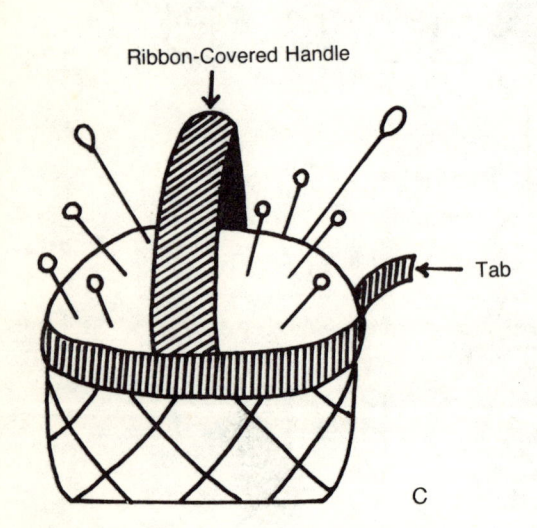

Photo Ashtray

Materials:

1 glass ashtray (from variety or department store)
1 photograph, the size of the base of the ashtray
white cement, paste-type that dries clear (craft store)
enamel paint, any color
fine brush
turpentine
rag
adhesive-backed felt, the size of the base of the ashtray

Method:

1. Place a fine line of cement all around the edge of the face of the photograph. Press the photograph to the outside base of the ashtray. Let dry.
2. Paint a design or message along the top rim of the ashtray. You may paint a border on the bottom of the ashtray, around the photograph.
3. Clean the brush, using the rag and turpentine, before storing.
4. Peel the backing off the felt and stick the felt to the base of the ashtray, on the back of the photograph.

Paperweight

Materials:

1 glass magnifying dome (from craft store)
1 piece of lightweight cardboard
pencil
scissors
adhesive-backed paper (craft store)
tiny dried or artificial flowers (craft store or florist)
florist clay (craft store or florist)
moss (craft store or florist)
felt-tipped pen, fine point, black
white glue that dries clear
toothpick
glitter (craft store)
white craft cement, paste-type (craft store)
adhesive-backed felt)

Method:

1. To make the base of the dome, place the glass dome on the cardboard and trace around it with a pencil. Cut out the pattern.
2. Place the cardboard pattern on the adhesive-backed paper and trace around it. Cut out the pattern, peel off the backing, and stick it to the cardboard.
3. With the pencil, write a holiday message on the paper-backed cardboard base, leaving room for the floral arrangement. Keep in mind that the entire design will be magnified. Place the dome on the base and check the lettering. Remove the dome.
4. Arrange the flowers on the base and secure with florist clay. Cover the clay with moss. Place the dome on the base and check the arrangement. Remove the dome.
5. Trace around the penciled lettering with the felt-tip pen.
6. Using the toothpick, apply a fine line of glue around the outline of each letter. Sprinkle glitter on the wet glue. Turn the base over to remove excess glitter.
7. Apply craft cement to the rim of the dome and place it on the completed base. Let dry.
8. Place the paperweight on the adhesive-backed felt and trace around it. Cut out the pattern, removing the backing, and stick it to the bottom of the paperweight.

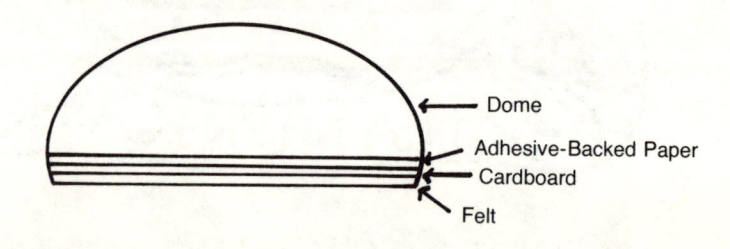

Wrap a Gift

After you have made a gift, put it in a container and wrap it. If the gift is large, you may want to decorate only the top of the package.

Almost any kind of paper may be used for wrapping. You may make Hanukkah designs on the wrapping with crayons, paint, or felt-tip pens.

Put your gift in:

shoe box
cigar box
matchbox
bandaid, aspirin, or pill tin
packing carton or crate
plastic berry basket

mailing tube
cardboard tube from paper towel
　　or toilet tissue roll
milk container
round oatmeal box
coffee tin with plastic lid
wood fruit crate

Wrap your gift in:

paper bags, cut open
drawing paper
fingerpaint paper
construction paper
typing paper
wax paper
heavy-duty household aluminum foil
tissue paper

metallic art paper
cellophane
paper toweling
paper place mats
paper tablecloth (for large gift)
wallpaper
newspaper section to suit receiver of gift
　　(sports, finance, recipes)
colored cartoon section from newspaper
fabric

More ideas for crafting decorated wrapping paper and gift boxes are presented in this section.

SIMPLE WRAPPING PAPER

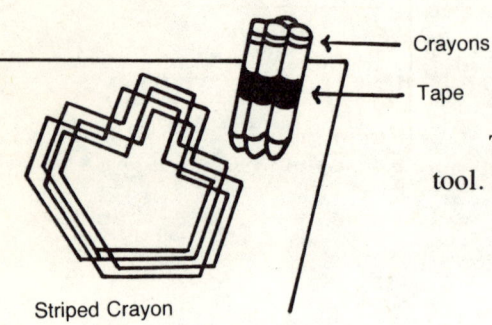

Striped Crayon Paper

Tape together several crayons, of assorted colors, to form a drawing tool. Using bold strokes, draw designs on the wrapping paper.

Paint-dabbed Paper

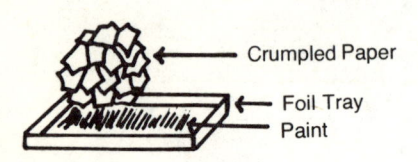

Make a disposable tray of heavy-duty household aluminum foil. Pour a little poster paint into the tray. Crumple a sheet of newspaper, dip it into the paint, and dab it all over the wrapping paper. Dip it in paint again when needed.

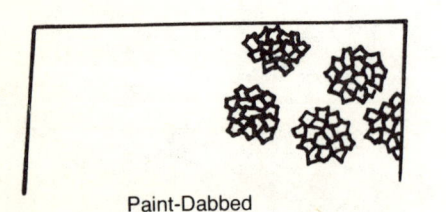

Handwriting Paper

With felt-tip pens, colored pencils, or crayons, write "Happy Hanukkah" in Hebrew or English all over one side of a sheet of paper.

Handprint Paper

Make a disposable tray of heavy-duty household aluminum foil. Brush fingerpaints on the bottom of the tray.

Flatten your open hand on the paint and then press down on the paper. Continue making as many handprints as you like. Let dry. With a felt-tip pen, write around the hands "Happy Hanukkah" and the name of the person receiving the gift.

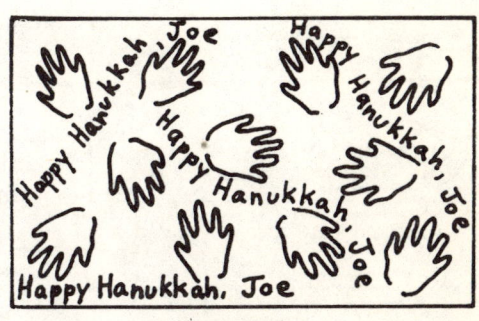

Handprint

Crayon and Wash Paper

Pressing firmly on brightly colored crayons, draw designs on one side of the paper. Thin black or dark blue poster paint with water.

Brush the "wash" over the entire colored side of the paper. The background will be dark and the crayoned areas will be bright.

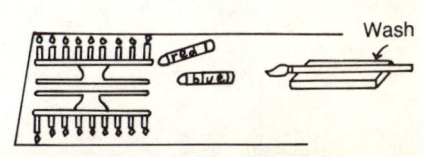

Crayon & Wash

Textured Paper

Paint a design on the paper. While the paint is still wet, sprinkle part of the design with glitter, colored sand, ground spices, or flaked or powdered soap. Let dry.

You may crayon the entire rough surface of coarse sandpaper. Cut out designs. Glue the cutouts to the wrapping paper.

Textured

Yarn-design Paper

Draw a design on the paper. Trace around the lines of the drawing with glue. Press yarn or cord along the glued lines. Let dry.

Yarn-Design

Doily-rubbing Paper

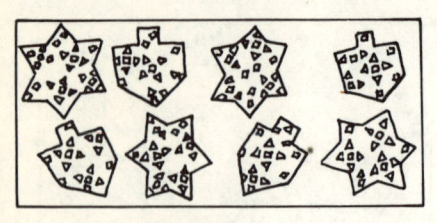

Cut a paper or plastic doily into shapes. Place paper over the doily shape and rub with a brightly colored crayon. Use a different color crayon for each shape.

Continue making rubbings until the entire paper is covered with designs.

Doily-Rubbing

Folded-and-dipped Wrapping Paper

Materials:

newspapers
sheet of absorbent paper (rice paper, easel paper, paper towels, or white tissue paper)

coloring agent (fabric dyes, food coloring, acrylics, or watercolor paint)

Folded & Dipped

Method:

1. Cover the work surface with newspapers. Fold the paper any way you choose, many times.
2. Dilute the coloring agent with water. Keep each color in a separate container.
3. Dip each corner of the folded paper into the coloring agent.
4. Carefully unfold the paper and place it on newspaper. Let dry.

Sprayed or Spattered Wrapping Paper

Materials:

newspapers
lightweight cardboard
scissors

wrapping paper
tempera paint
spray bottle

Optional: old toothbrush, stick

Method:

1. Cover the work surface with newspapers. Cut out Hanukkah symbols from lightweight cardboard. Arrange the cutouts on the wrapping paper.
2. Thin the paint with water if it is too thick.
3. Pour the paint into a spray bottle and spray the paper, going right over the cutouts. Make sure the cutouts remain in place. You may dip a toothbrush into the paint instead. Spatter paint over the paper by drawing a stick toward you across the bristles. Let dry.
4. Remove the cutouts. The spaces covered by the cutouts will remain the original color of the paper.

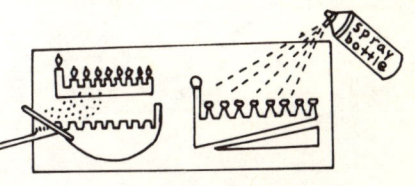

Sprayed or Spattered

Ink-and-string-painted Wrapping Paper

Materials:

newspapers
heavy-duty household aluminum foil
ink, any colors
string
scissors
wrapping paper

Optional: crayons, paint, or felt-tip pens, book

Ink-and-String-Painted

Method:

1. Cover the work surface with newspapers. Make a disposable tray of foil. Pour a little ink into the tray. Use a different tray for each color ink.
2. Cut about two feet of string for each color ink used. Hold one end of the string and dip it into the ink.
3. Place the string on the wrapping paper in a random design. Lift the string off the paper. Keep inking and "placing" the string until the entire paper is printed.
4. Some of the designed areas may be colored with crayons, paint, or felt-tip pens.
5. To make a blurred mirror-image print, place inked strings on one paper. One end of each string must hang off the paper. Cover this with another paper and on top of this a book. Hold the book in place with one hand. Using your other hand, wiggle each string, or pull it from side to side until it comes free. When all the strings have been pulled, remove the book and separate the two printed papers. Place the papers on newspaper. Let dry.

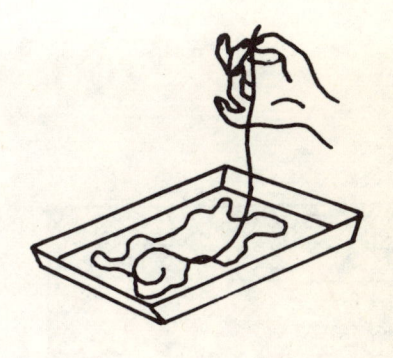

Crumpled Paper

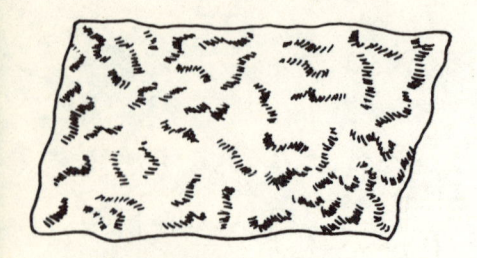

Cover the work surface with newspapers. Wet a sheet of paper, then crumple it and uncrumple it.

Brush the entire surface of one side of the paper with watercolor paint. Quickly pass the paper under running tap water.

All the paint will wash off, except the paint in the creases. Place the paper on newspapers and let dry.

Crumpled

Layered Color Paper

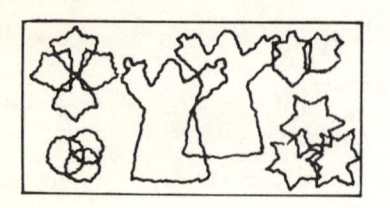

Tear colored tissue paper into shapes. Overlap the shapes on the paper, creating new color combinations.

Glue the shapes to the paper by brushing liquid starch, white glue thinned with water, or acrylic polymer medium over the surface of the paper. Let dry.

Layered Color

Cement-printed Paper

Using rubber cement, outline designs on paper. Let dry.

Brush the surface of the paper with watercolor or tempera paint. Let dry.

With your fingers, rub the cement-covered areas. This will remove both the paint and the cement, leaving the original color of the paper with a pretty, mottled look. With a felt-tip pen, outline the designs.

Cement-Printed

Marbled Paper

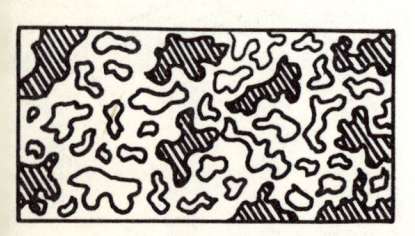

Brush oil paint over one side of the wrapping paper. Place a sheet of clear plastic wrap on the wet paper. Press your fingers on different parts of the wrap.

Peel the wrap off the paper. The painted surface will appear marbled. Let dry.

Marbled

DECORATED GIFT BOXES

Hanukkah Card Cutout Box

Cut designs and printed lettering from old Hanukkah cards. Arrange the cutouts and glue to the gift box.

Hanukkah Card Cutout

Fabric-covered Box

Wrap the box and the box top with solid color fabric or paper. Glue on scraps of fabric and fabric trim.

Fabric-Covered

Painted Box

To cover any printing, brush on a base coat of gesso (from craft store). Let dry. Apply a second coat if needed and let dry.

Draw a design on the box top. The design may run down the sides of the box. With tempera or acrylic paint, fill in the design. Let dry.

Painted

MORE WRAPPING PAPER

Inkblot Paper

Start with an absorbent sheet of paper. Fold in thirds, as shown by the dotted lines in figure A. Unfold.

Using one or more colors of ink, drip small blobs along the creased lines. Refold the paper along the original creases (figure B).

To spread the ink, press along the folds, using your fist in some areas, your palm in other areas, and also your fingertips. Unfold and let dry (figure C).

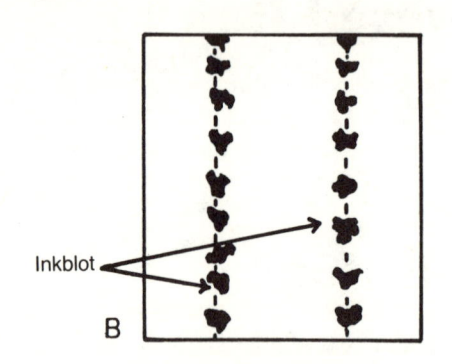

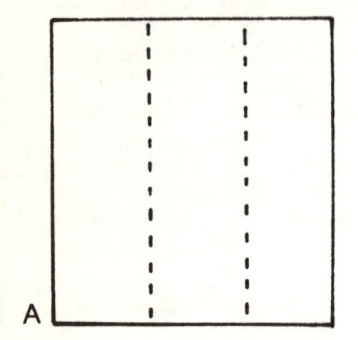

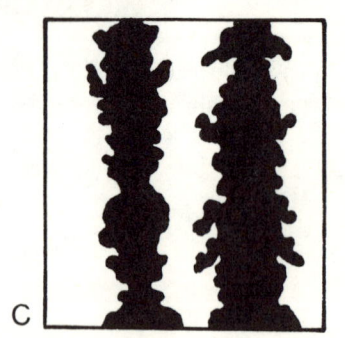

Straw-Painted

Straw-painted Paper

Place a few large drops of poster paint on the lower part of the paper. Thin the paint with water if it is too thick. Hold a plastic drinking straw almost on the level of the paper, behind the drops of paint. Blow through the straw and the paint will fan out, forming branch-like designs.

Soap or Wax Print Paper

Start with a bar of soap or paraffin (from supermarket) or a wax block (craft store). Carve a design into it with an open paper clip, nail file, or toothpick.

Make a disposable tray of heavy-duty household aluminum foil. Pour a little poster paint into the tray.

Dip the carved side of the soap or wax block into the paint, then press onto the paper. Continue printing until the paper is covered. Let dry.

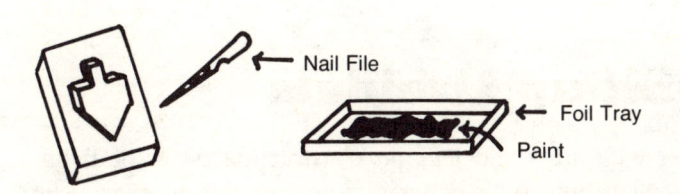

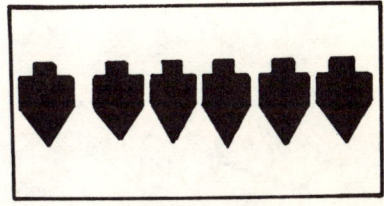

← Nail File

← Foil Tray
Paint

Soap or Wax Print

Fingerprints Paper

To print, press a finger firmly on an inked stamp pad and then on the paper.

Use your little finger for small areas and your thumb for larger areas. Experiment with each of your fingers, sometimes on the tip, the side, or the full finger.

Add a few strokes of a felt-tip pen to turn the prints into a dreidel, Star of David, menorah, flower, bird, or butterfly.

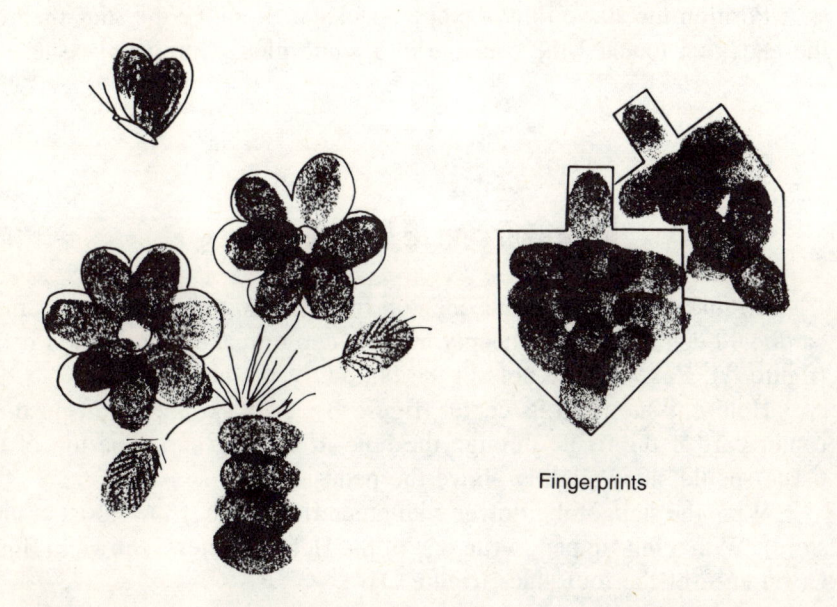

Fingerprints

PACKAGE DECORATIONS

Sit-up Dreidels

Draw a dreidel with arms and legs on construction paper or lightweight cardboard. Cut it out. With crayons, paint, or felt-tip pens, add facial features and other details. Fold the dreidel into a sitting position. Place along the edge of the wrapped package and glue in place. Let dry.

Three-dimensional Stars

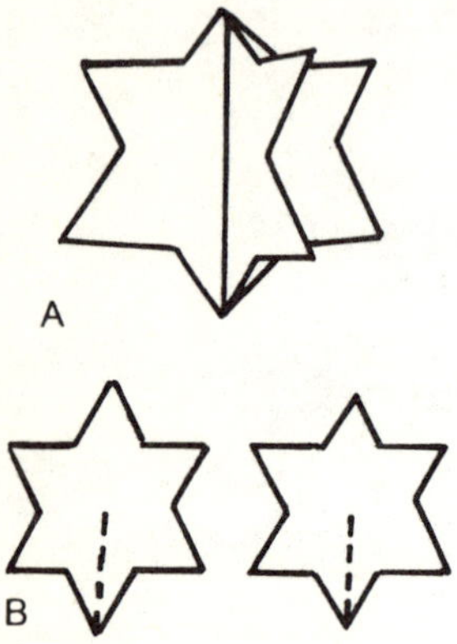

Cut two identical Stars of David out of thin cardboard, construction paper, styrofoam meat trays, or aluminum foil pie plates.

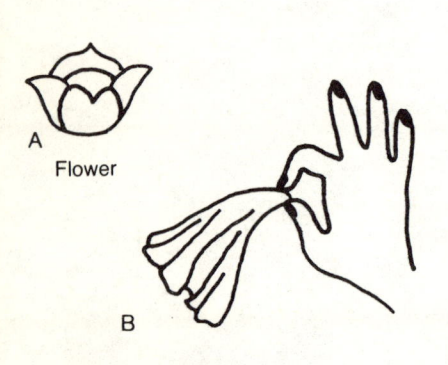

Cut a slit going halfway up the center of each symbol, as shown by the dotted lines in figure A. To assemble, slide the cut portions of each symbol into each other (figure B).

Position the star on the wrapped package. Remove the star, then dip the ends that touched the package into white glue. Glue in place and let dry.

Flower Dreidels

To make one flower, cut one cup from the bottom of a styrofoam or cardboard egg carton. Cut deeply into the cup to make four pointed petals (figure A). Poke a large hole in the bottom of the egg cup.

Hold a tissue from its center (figure B). To make the stem, push the center part of the tissue through the hole in the egg cup. The top of the tissue should show slightly above the petals.

Wrap the stem of the flower with green floral tape (from florist or craft store). With a felt-tip pen, write one of the Hebrew letters, shown in figure C, on each of the four sides (figure D).

Repeat to make more flowers. Glue the flowers to the wrapped package. Let dry.

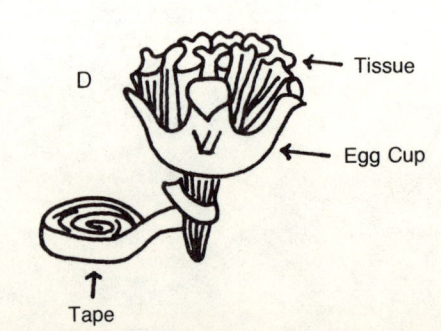

Send a Card

Wish your friends and family a "Happy Hanukkah" by sending cards and adding them to gift packages. The traditional greeting is

חג חנוכה שמח

Make personalized cards, using the ideas in this section. Be sure to write a message inside in the card, sign your name, and insert in an envelope.

Simple Cards

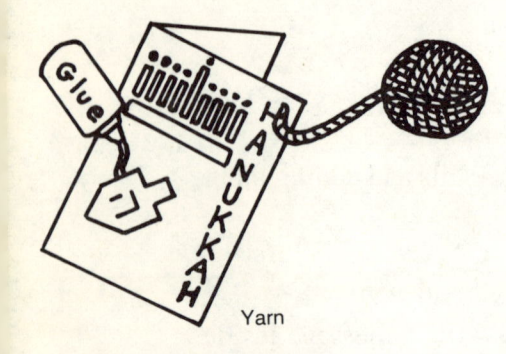

YARN CARD

Fold a sheet of paper in half. Write a message or draw a picture inside the card. Draw a simple Hanukkah picture on the front of the card. Trace with glue the lines of the design. Press colored yarn on the glued lines.

MOCK STAINED GLASS CARD

Fold a sheet of paper in half. Write a message or draw a picture inside the card.

On the cover of the card, pencil in designs to look like stained glass. Trace with a broad point black felt-tip pen the lines of the design. Fill in the designs with felt-tip pens in other colors.

FOIL-BACKED WINDOW CARD

Fold a sheet of dark construction paper, 6" × 12," in half. Write a message or draw a picture inside the card.

Draw a design on lighter color construction paper, 2½" × 5½", and cut out. Cut household aluminum foil to the same size as the lighter construction paper.

Glue the foil behind the lighter color construction paper so the foil shows through the cutouts. Mount on the cover of the folded construction paper.

Yarn

Mock Stained Glass

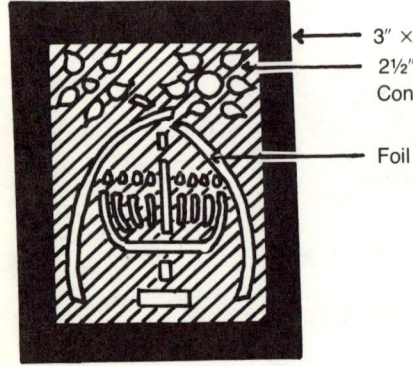

Foil Backed Window

- 3" × 6" Dark Construction Paper
- 2½" × 5½" Lighter Color Construction Paper
- Foil

Button People Card

Materials:

construction paper, 6" × 6", any color
pencil
white buttons, each with 2 holes
white glue
felt-tip pens, any color
fabric scraps
yarn scraps
envelope, 3⅝" × 6½"

Method:

1. Fold the paper in half.
2. On the front of the folded card, pencil in a design that includes "button people."
3. Place the buttons on the card, using the two holes as eyes, and glue down.
4. Draw eyebrows and a mouth with the pens. Add clothing by gluing on

scraps of fabric. Add hair by gluing on yarn.
5. Trace over the penciled lines with the pens.
6. Write a Hanukkah message inside the card. Insert in an envelope. With the pens, add a border of color to the envelope.

Button People

Crayon Lift-off Card

Materials:

white bond paper, 6" × 6"
pencil
crayons, various colors, including black
chalk
envelope, 3⅝" × 6½"

Optional: felt-tip pens, any colors

Method:

1. Fold the paper in half to form a card. Pencil a Hanukkah message on the front of the card (figure A). Color the design with crayons or felt-tip pens.
2. Heavily coat the left side of the inside of the card with chalk.
3. Coat the chalked area with a thick layer of crayon.
4. Close the card and turn it so the back faces up. Pressing heavily on the pencil, draw a Hanukkah picture on the back. Open the card. The

crayon will have been lifted off the left side of the inside and will appear on the right side in the pencil design you have drawn (figure B).

5. Sign your name and insert in an envelope.

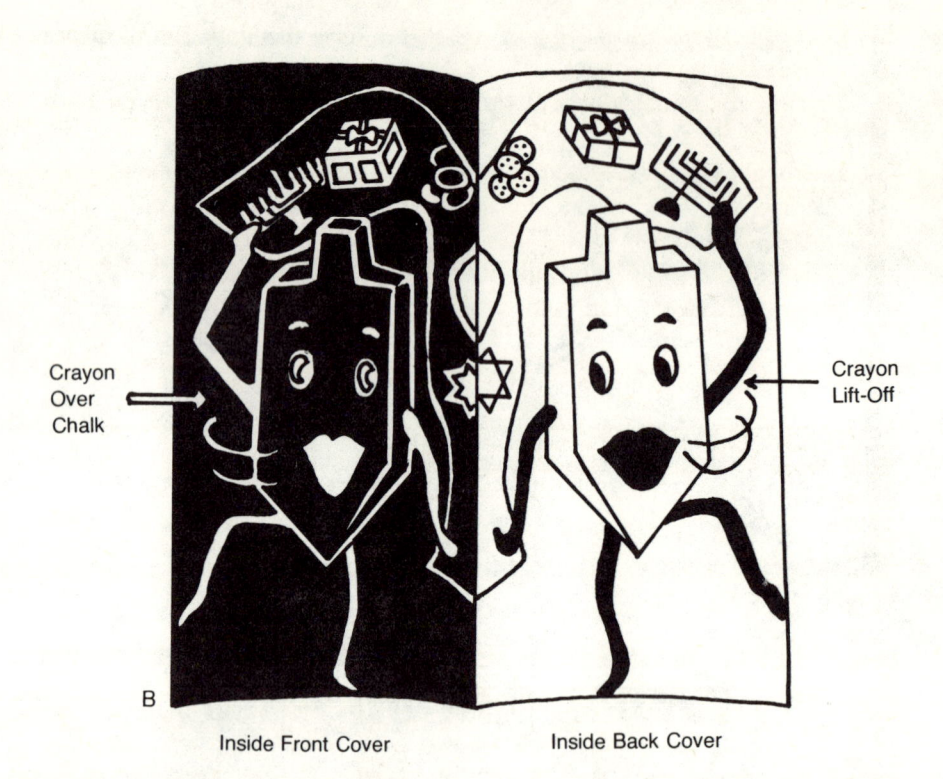

A Front Cover

B Inside Front Cover   Inside Back Cover

Crayon Over Chalk

Crayon Lift-Off

Hole-punch Card

Materials:

1 sheet of construction paper, 6" × 6", dark color
1 sheet of construction paper, 5½" × 5½", light color
hole punch
pencil
felt-tip pens, any colors
white glue
wax paper
straight pin
toothpick
envelope, 3⅝" × 6½"

Method:

1. Fold the dark sheet of paper in half.
2. Punch evenly spaced holes all around the edge of the light color paper. Save the punched-out circles. Fold the paper in half.
3. Pencil a design on the front of the light color construction paper.
4. With the felt-tip pens, color in the penciled design.
5. Glue the light color construction paper over the dark folded paper (figure A).
6. Arrange the punched-out circles in a design on the inside of the card (figure B).
7. Pour a glob of white glue onto a piece of wax paper. Stick the pin into one of the punched-out circles. With the toothpick, dab a dot of glue on the underside of the circle (figure C) and place it back in the design. Continue until all circles are glued in place.
8. Write a message, sign your name, and insert in an envelope.

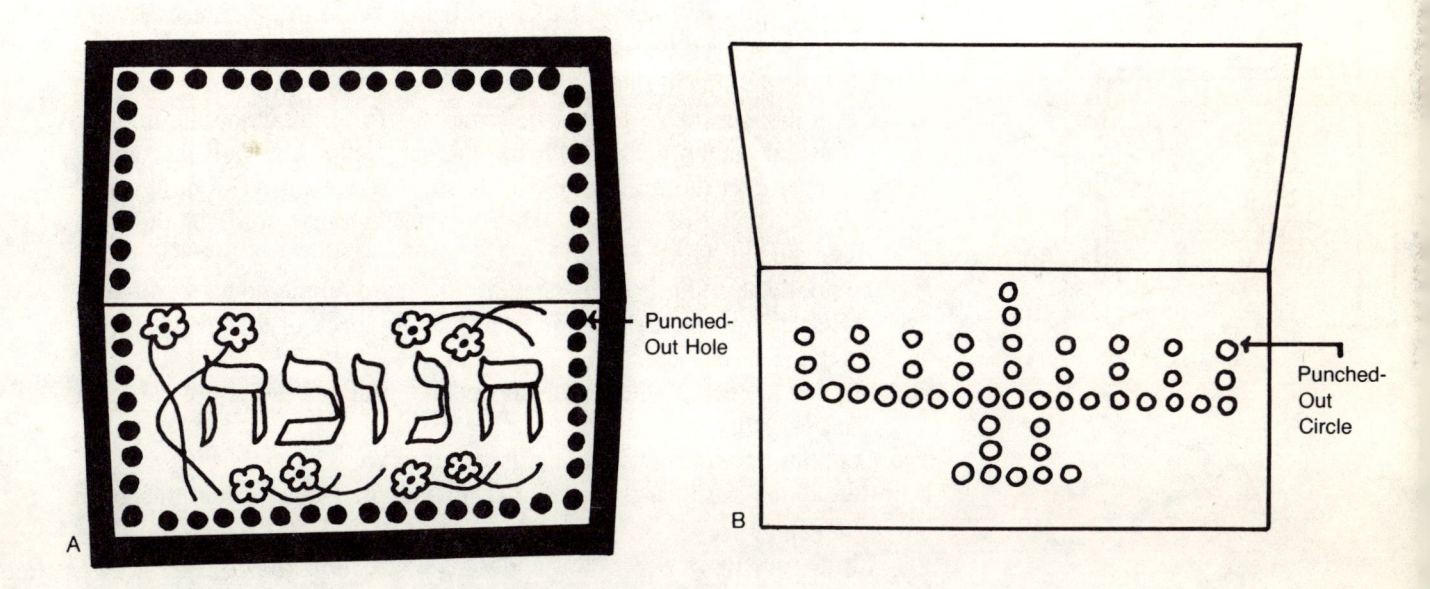

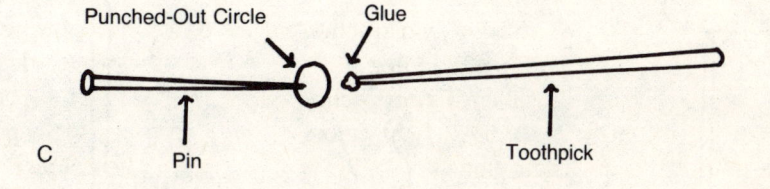

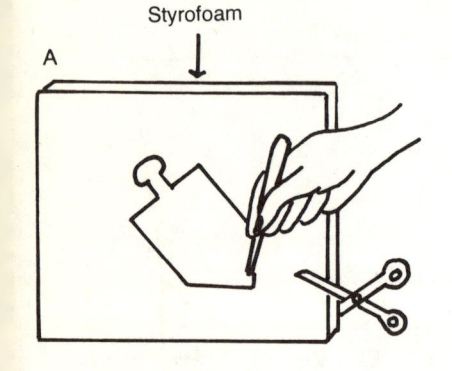

Relief-printed Cards

Materials:

sheets of bond or construction paper, each 3" × 10", any colors
2 pieces of styrofoam, each 3" × 5" (from craft store or cut-up supermarket meat trays)
pencil
scissors
glue
newspapers
water-soluble ink, any color (craft store)
brayer (craft store)
household aluminum foil, shaped into a shallow pan
wooden spoon
envelopes, 3⅝" × 6½"

Method:

1. Fold a sheet of paper in half, to measure 3" × 5". Unfold the paper.
2. Draw designs on one piece of styrofoam. Avoid using letters because they will print backwards. Cut out each design (figure A).
3. Glue the designs to the second piece of styrofoam (figure B). Let dry.
4. Cover the work surface with newspapers. To print, spoon ink into the foil pan and roll thin with the brayer (figure C). Roll the coated brayer over the printing block of glued styrofoam. The design will be the color of the ink, while the background color of the card remains as it was.
5. To print, place the front of one unfolded card on the inked styrofoam. Rub the reverse side of the front with the back of the spoon (figure D).
6. Lift one corner of the paper and gently peel off the styrofoam. Set aside to dry.
7. Continue printing as many cards as you like.
8. Refold the cards and write a Hanukkah message inside. Insert in envelopes.
9. Clean your tools with water and dry them before storing.

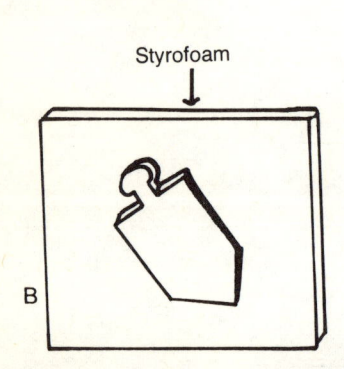

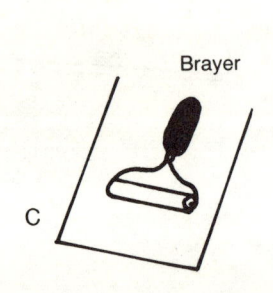

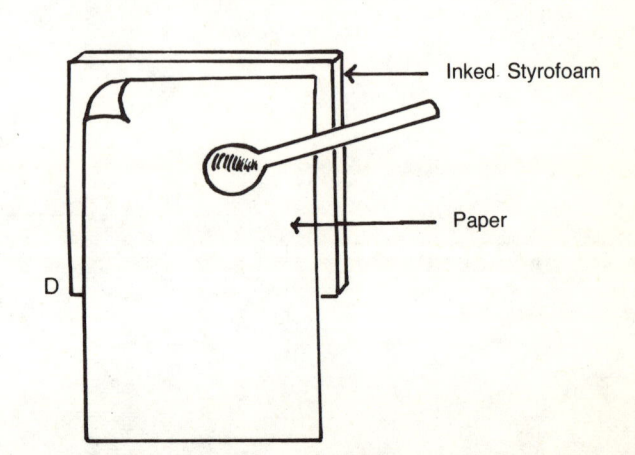

Linoleum-block Printed Cards

Materials:

sheets of thin paper, 3″ × 5″, any color
pencil
masking tape
carbon paper
linoleum block, 3″ × 5″ (from craft store)
several cutting tools: thin, wide, V-shaped gouges (craft store)
water-soluble ink, any color
aluminum foil tray
brayer (craft store)
sheets of white paper, each 3″ × 10″
wooden spoon
envelopes, each 3⅝″ × 6½″

Method:

1. To make the design for the card, draw a design on a sheet of thin paper (figure A). Tape the paper to a window with the designed side against the window. The light shining through the paper will enable you to see the drawing on the reverse side. Trace over the lines of this drawing. The picture is now reversed, which will prevent any words you have drawn from printing backwards later.
2. To transfer the design, put carbon paper, face up, on the linoleum block. Then place the thin paper on top, with the reverse side of the picture facing you. Tape to hold (figure B). Trace the lines of the design; when you print, the design will be right side up. Remove the tape, carbon paper, and picture.
3. Shade all areas on the thin paper that you will want to cut away (figure C). (To prevent accidents when you cut, keep your free hand in back of your cutting tool—it is sharp.)
4. To texture the linoleum block, outline the picture with a small V-shaped gouge. Use the small cutting tools for details and the

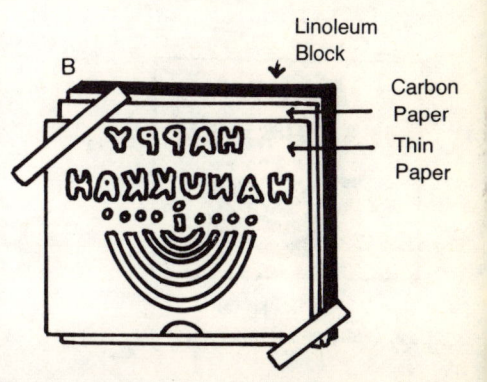

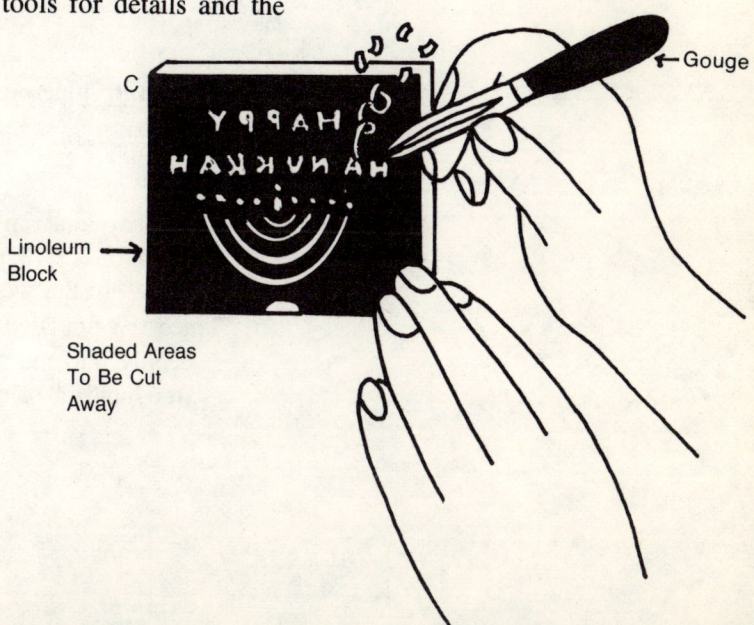

Brayer

D

Wooden Spoon

E

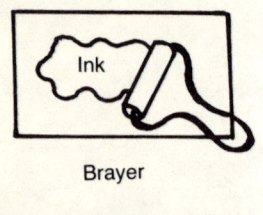

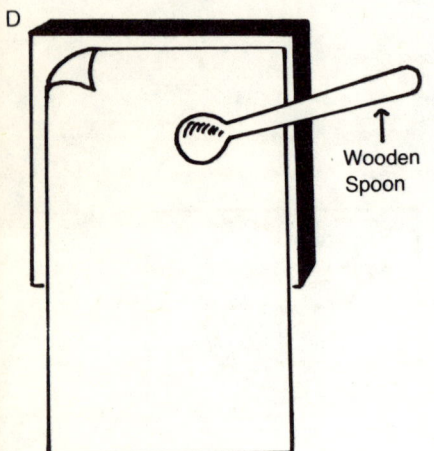

HAPPY HANUKKAH

Tooled Background Remains White

wider ones for broad areas. You may cut away the background, leaving the picture raised, or cut out the picture, leaving the background raised. On the printed card, the tooled area will remain white (figure E).

5. Cover the work surface with newspapers. To make one card, fold a sheet of white paper in half to measure 3" × 5". Unfold the paper. To print the card, spoon ink into the foil tray and roll it with the brayer until it is thin and even. Roll the coated brayer over the cut block, making sure the block is completely and evenly coated with ink.
6. Place the front of the unfolded card on the inked block and carefully hold it in place. Rub the reverse side with the back of the spoon (figure D).
7. Lift one corner of the card and peel off the block. Set aside to dry.
8. Continue printing as many cards as you like.
9. Clean the tools before storing.
10. Refold each card (figure E). Write a Hanukkah message and sign your name inside. Insert in an envelope.

Wood-block Printed Cards

Materials:

scrap block of soft wood, pine or other, 3" × 5" (from lumber yard or builder)
pencil
cutting tool (small skewer, long nail, pointed end of a soda can opener, screwdriver, or tip of scissors)
newspapers

sheet of household aluminum foil (edges bent up to form a tray)
water-soluble ink, any color
brayer (craft store)
sheets of white bond or construction paper, each 3" × 10"
wooden spoon
envelopes, each 3⅝" × 6½"

Optional: glue-on picture hanger

Method:

1. On the wood scrap, draw a design to fit one folded card, about 3" × 5". Words will print backwards unless written backwards (figure A). Hold the wood block up to a mirror to check the lettering.
2. Trace the penciled lines of the design with a cutting tool, pressing deeply into the wood (figure A). To prevent accidents, keep your free hand in back of the cutting tool—it is sharp.

3. Cover the work surface with newspapers. Spoon ink into the foil pan and roll it thin and even with the brayer (figure B). Roll the coated brayer over the surface of the wood, making sure it is completely and evenly coated with ink.
4. Place the front of the unfolded card on the inked block. Rub the reverse side of the front with the back of the spoon (figure C).
5. Take one corner of the card and carefully peel off the block. Set aside to dry.
6. Continue printing as many cards as you like.
7. You may wash the ink off the wood or leave it. When the ink dries, use the block as a standing decoration or attach a picture hanger and hang.
8. Clean the tools before storing.
9. Refold the card (figure D) and write a Hanukkah message inside. Insert in an envelope.

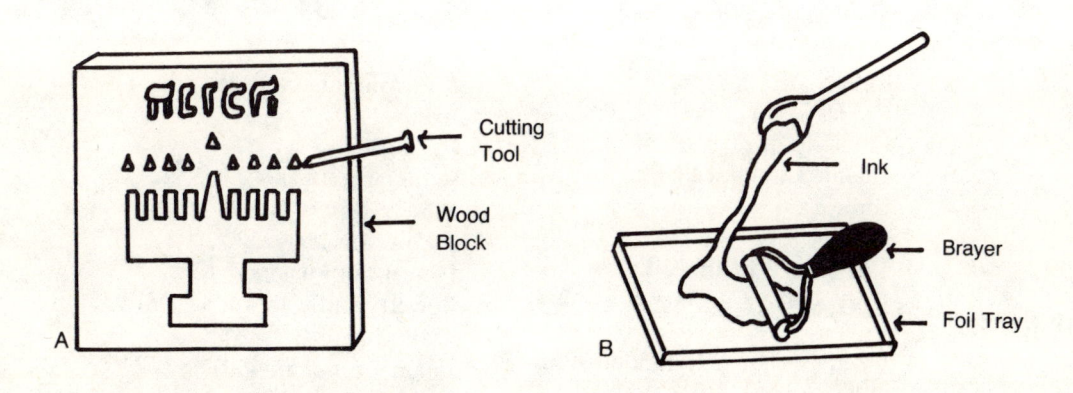

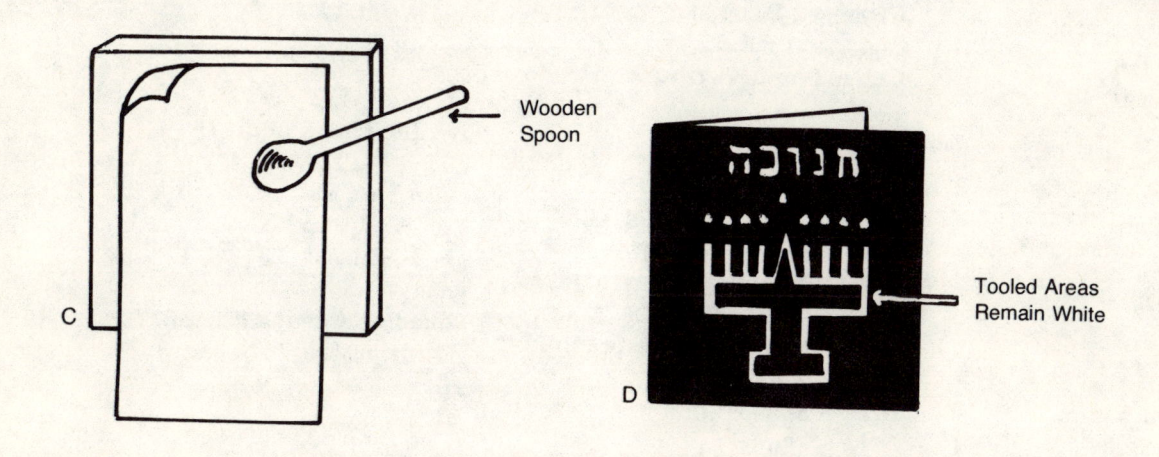

Index

A

Acrylic Painted Decanter, 87
adding machine tape, 44
adhesives
    candle, 12, 14, 17
    floral, 12, 14, 17
aluminum sheet, 88
ashtray, glass, 119

B

Ball-in-the-dreidel Cup Game, 66
Balloon Candy Holder, 58
Basket Pincushion, 118
basket, wicker, 96
Bead Mezuzah, 80
beads, 23, 28, 38, 80, 110
Beanbag Party Favor, 57
beeswax, 25
bell, 98
Bleach Out a Tablecloth Design, 43, 44
blocks, 17, 24, 28, 47
Bookcovers, 95
Bookmarks, 94
Bookplates, 96
Bottle Doll, 40
brayer, 136–138
Bright Crayon Mizrah, 90
Bulletin Board, 116
Burlap Napkin Rings, 48
burs, 102
Bur Tree Picture, 102
butterflies, pressed, 95
Button People Card, 132, 133

C

cactus plants, 103, 104
Candleholder Menorah, 17
candleholders, metal, 17
candles, 88, 117
    Hanukkah, 12–19, 22, 23, 24

candy holders, 58–60
Cardboard Box Movie Theater, 74
Cardboard Box Stage, 78
Cardboard Puppet, 75
Cartoon Mural, **31,** 32
Cement-printed Paper, 126
chenille craftsticks, 37, 58
clay
    air-hardening, 13, 83
    florist, 96, 120
    kiln-hardening, 13
    non-hardening, 13
    oven-hardening, 13, 28, 83
Clay Dreidel, 28
Clay Menorot, 13
Clay Mezuzah, 83, 84
Clothespin Menorah, 22
Clothespin Puppet, 77
coins, foil-covered chocolate, **7,** 55, 56, 58, 60
Collage Mizrah, 89
Colored Sand Planter, 104, 105
Comic Strip Bookmark, 94
Cookie Container, 100
cork, 35, 111
    sheet, 21, 102, 116
Corkboard Picture, 35
Corrugated Cardboard Symbol, 33, 34
Costumes for a Hanukkah Play, 72
cotton batting, 38, 101
Craft-plaster Necklace, 108
Crayon and Wash Paper, 123
Crayon Lift-off Card, 133, 134
Crayon-rubbing Mizrah, 89
Crumpled Paper, 126
cups, paper nut, 12
Cut-and-paste Puzzle, 66, 67

D

"Dinner's On" Bell Pull, 98
Doily-rubbing Paper, 124
Doorknob Do-not-disturb Sign, 97
dowels, 28, 29, 35, 75, 77
Dreidel Game Party Favor, 56
Dreidel Nut Toss, 65
Dreidel Spinner, 68
dreidels, 56, 60
dressmaker's carbon, 36, 43, 85, 91
dyes, 46, 124

E

Egg Carton Dreidel, 28
Egg Carton Jewelry Box, 109
Egg-shaped Menorah, 19, 20
Egg-shell Mosaic Mizrah, 90
Embroidered Mat, 36
Embroidered Mizrah, 91
embroidery floss, 36, 86, 91
embroidery hoop, 91
embroidery needles, 36, 91
eyes, movable, 39, 98

F

Fabric-covered Box, 127
felt, adhesive-backed, 119, 120
Fingerprints Paper, 129
Finger Puppets, 76
fishing line, 108
Five Maccabees on Parade, The, 39
fixative, 89
Floral Bookcover, 95
floral tape, 130
Flower Basket Bookend, 96
Flower Dreidels, 130
Flower Pot Menorah, 12
flowers, artificial, 40, 48, 58, 95, 96, 120
Foam Cutout Invitations, 52
Foil-backed Window Card, 132
Folded-and-dipped Wrapping Paper, 124
frames, 49, 91

G

gesso, 87, 127
Get the Latkes in the Oven, 62
glitter, 44, 120, 123
glitter glue, 98
gouges, V-shaped, 137
gravel, colored, 33
grout, 50
Gumdrop Candy Menorah, 16
gelt, Hanukkah, **7,** 8, 55, 58, 60

H

Hand-dipped Hanukkah Candles, 26

Hand Jewelry Holder, 111
Hand-painted Kippah, 85
Handpainted Soap, 117
Handprint Paper, 123
Hand-rolled Hanukkah Candles, 25
Hand-sewn Kippah, 86
Handwriting Paper, 122
Hanukkah Card Cutout Box, 127
Hanukkah Hop Game, 64
Hanukkah Number Game, 70
Hanukkah Word Game, 69
Hole-punch Card, 134, 135
Holiday Napkin Holder, 47
House-shaped Invitations, 53

I

Ink-and-string-painted Wrapping Paper, 125
Inkblot Paper, 128
Instant Papier-mâché Mezuzah, 81
iron-on
    fusible material, 112
    tape, 114
Israeli flag picks, 39

J

jump ring, 108

K

key chain, metal, 107
kippot, 84–86
klaf, **79,** 80–83

L

Label for Wine Decanter, 88
labels, mailing, 96
Laced Plastic Napkin Rings, 48
Layered Color Paper, 126
leather lace, 86
leaves, artificial, 40, 95
Lend-a-hand Potholder, 101
Light-the-menorah Game, 63
linoleum block, 137
Linoleum-block Printed Cards, 137, 138

liquid embroidery, 36, 86, 88, 101

M

Macaroni Star, 33
Maccabee Candy Holder, 60
Magnetic "Put-ons," 98
magnetic sheet, 98
magnifying dome, glass, 120
Marbled Paper, 126
Matchbox Mezuzah, 80
Melted Crayon Bookcover, 95
mezuzot, 79–84
Mixed-medium Mizrah, 89
mizrahim, 89–91
Mock Pomander Dreidel, 34–35
Mock Stained Glass Card, 132
Mock Stained Glass Decanter, 87
Mock Stained Glass Mizrah, 90
Modeled Head Puppet, 77
modeling paste, acrylic polymer, 110
Mosaic Tray, 50
moss, dried, 96, 120

N

Napkin Rings, 48
necklace, 108
Nut Jewelry, 108

O

Oil Menorah, 21

P

Paint-dabbed Paper, 122
Painted Box, 127
Paint-sample Bookmarks, 94
paint-sample chart, 94
palette knife, 15
paper, adhesive-backed, 45, 94, 95, 97, 100, 120
Paper Circle Mizrah, 90
Paper Cup Candy Holders, 58
Paper Cup Menorah, 12
Paper Cutout Tablecloth, 42
Paper Kippah, 84

Paper Symbol Chain, 32
Paperweight, 120
papier-mâché, 77, 81
paraffin, 127
Pencil-painted Mizrah, 89
People Bookmark, 94
Photo Ashtray, 119
Photo in Plastic, 106
Picture–frame Recipe Tray, 48, 49
Pin the Shield on Judah Maccabee, 63
Ping Pong Ball Dreidel, 28
Pinprick Bookcover, 95
Pins, 108
Pipe Cleaner Picture, 37
Place Cards, 54
Place Marker and Party Favor, 55
Plaster Cast Menorah, 18, 19
plaster of Paris, 19, 38, 103
plaster, powdered craft, 18, 108
Plastic Covered Place Mats, 45
Plastic Pill Bottle Mezuzah, 80
plastic sheets, 106
plastic spray, 81, 102, 108
Popsicle Stick Puppet, 75
Poster Board Dreidel, 30
Puppet Theaters, 78
putty knife, 15

R

Rag Doll Rod Puppet, 77
Relief-printed Cards, 136
Ribbon Bookmark, 94
ribbon straw, 48
Ribbon-straw Napkin Rings, 48
rickrack, 94, 98
rug tape, 36

S

sand, 12, 24, 38, 104, 123
Sand-cast Menorah, 38
seashell, 82
Seashell Mezuzah, 82, 83
shamash, **11**
Shadow Puppet, 77
Shadow Puppet Stage, 78
Shoe Box Movie Theater, 74
Shoe Planter, 103

Shrinking Plastic Key Holder, 107
Simple Cards, 132
Simple Decorations, 32
Simple Dreidels, 28
Simple Menorot, 12
Simple Mezuzot, 80
Simple Mizrahim, 89
Simple Wine Decanters, 87
Simple Wrapping Paper, 122
Sit-up Dreidels, 130
Soap or Wax Print Paper, 127
soil, potting, 104
spackle, 15
Spackle Menorah, 15
Spool Menorah, 23
Spool Mezuzah, 80
Sports Patches, 114
Sprayed or Spattered Wrapping Paper, 124, 125
stain
   glass, 21, 40
   wood, 82
Standing Dreidel, 32
Stapled Cardboard Dreidel, 29
Straw-painted Paper, 128
Striped Crayon Paper, 122

styrofoam, 15, 60
   ball, 34, 37, 40, 66, 75, 100
   block, 14, 111
   cone, 75
   egg, 110
   ring, 40
   tray, 37, 52, 136
Styrofoam Cone and Ball Puppet, 75
Styrofoam-egg Jewelry Box, 110
Sweat Towel, 112

T

tablecloth, paper, 42
Tablecloth Runners, 44, 45
Tape and Shoe-polish Decanter, 87
Test Tube Menorah, 24
test tubes, 24
Textured Paper, 123
Textured Wine Bottle, 88
Thimble Menorah, 14
thimbles, 14
3-cord crochet, 58
Three-dimensional Stars, 130
Tie-dyed Place Mats, 46
tile cement, 50
tiles, 50

Tissue-twist Holder, 59
Toothpick and Button Dreidel, 28

V

varnish, 16-18, 22-24

W

Wallpaper Bookmark, 94
Watercolor and Pen Mizrah, 89
wax, 26, 117, 127
   cold, 43
wax coloring, 26
Wheel with a Collar Dreidel, 28
Whittled Walking Stick, 102
wicks, 21, 25, 26
Window Mizrah, 90
wine decanters, 87, 88
Wood-block Printed Cards, 138, 139
Wood Mezuzah, 82

Y

Yarn Card, 132
Yarn-design Paper, 123

ABOUT THE BOOK

As in her best-selling JEWISH HOLIDAY CRAFTS, Joyce Becker provides easy-to-follow illustrated instructions for over 200 colorful and useful objects. The all-new projects in HANUKKAH CRAFTS range from very easy to very challenging, with something of interest for the beginner, as well as the experienced craftsperson, of any age. Introductory notes explain the history and customs of the holiday—everything you need to know about Hanukkah.

Children, teenagers, and adults can share the fun of making and giving gifts, having a Hanukkah party, and putting on a show. Candles and cards, dolls and decorations, puppets and games add to the festivity. The imaginative projects make use of readily available, inexpensive materials to enhance the holiday. Many of the handcrafted original gift items will bring pleasure all through the year.

HANUKKAH CRAFTS is an ideal personal gift and an indispensable reference for classrooms, libraries, and community centers.

ABOUT THE AUTHOR

Joyce Becker has tested every project in HANUKKAH CRAFTS on family and friends, as well as in the creative art classes she has taught on all age levels during the past seven years.

Mrs. Becker's teaching experience includes crafts classes for the mentally retarded at Woodbridge State School in New Jersey. She studied at Pratt Institute and has written and illustrated greeting cards. She is a member of the Writers' Association of New Jersey. Her first published book was the widely-acclaimed JEWISH HOLIDAY CRAFTS.

Joyce Becker lives in Edison, New Jersey with her husband and their four children.

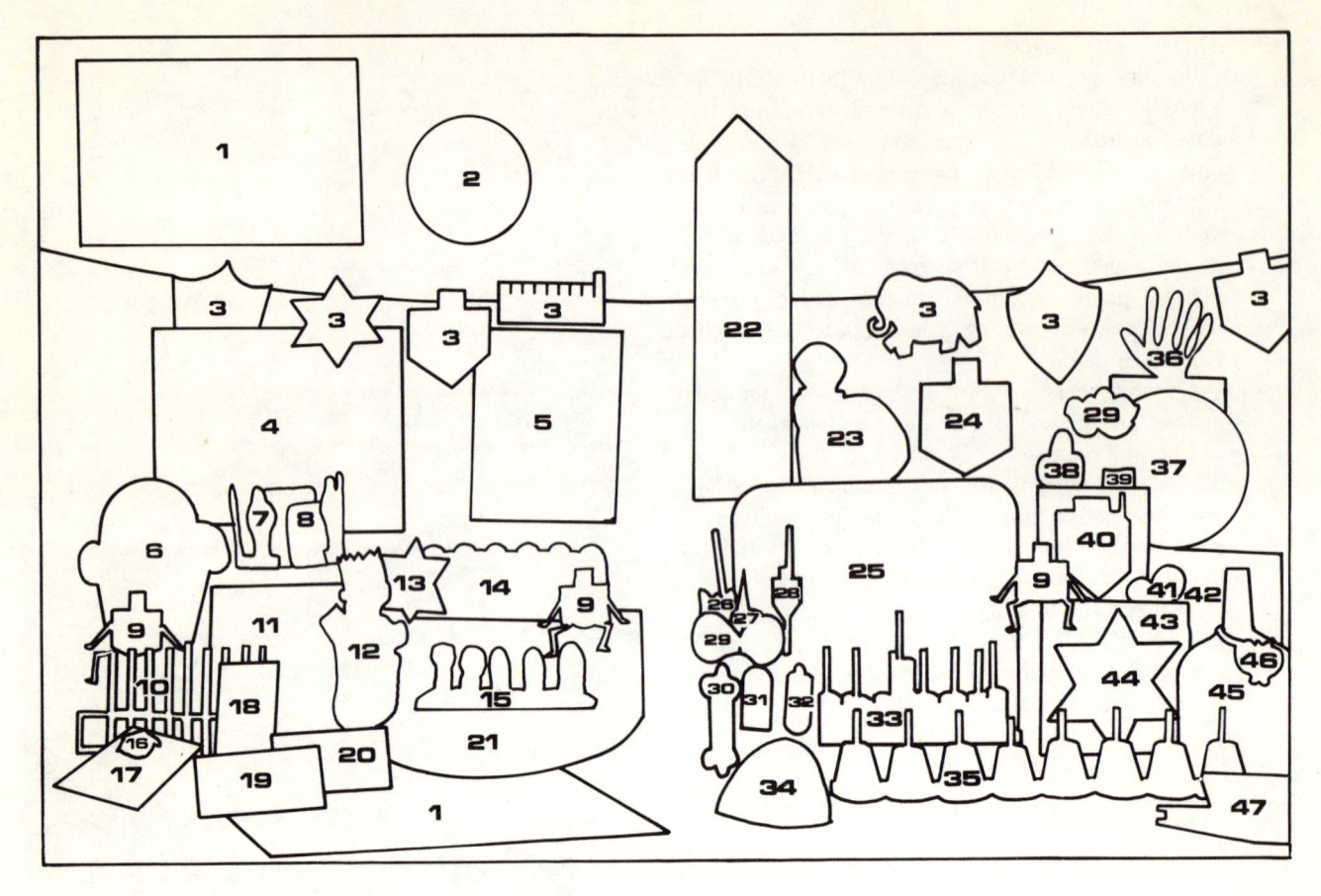

key to cover photo

1. Crayon and Wash Wrapping Paper
2. Magnetic "Put-Ons"
3. Paper Symbol Chain
4. Picture Frame Recipe Tray
5. Cut-and-Paste Puzzle
6. Flower Basket Bookend
7. Maccabee Candy Holder
8. Handpainted Soap
9. Sit-Up Dreidel
10. Test Tube Menorah
11. Doily Rubbing Wrapping Paper
12. Modeled Head Puppet
13. Three-dimensional Star
14. Egg Carton Jewelry Box
15. The Five Maccabees on Parade
16. Shrinking Plastic Key Holder
17. Doorknob Do-Not-Disturb Sign
18. Foil-backed Window Card
19. Button People Card
20. Hole-punch Card
21. Clothespin Menorah
22. "Dinner's On" Bell Pull
23. Bottle Doll
24. Mock Pomander Dreidel
25. Mosaic Tray
26. Egg Carton Dreidel
27. Ping Pong Ball Dreidel
28. Stapled Cardboard Dreidel
29. Flower Dreidels
30. Clay Mezuzah
31. Seashell Mezuzah
32. Bead Mezuzah
33. Spool Menorah
34. Hand-painted Kippah
35. Flower Pot Menorah
36. Hand Jewelry Holder
37. Dreidel Spinner
38. Basket Pincushion
39. Ribbon Straw Napkin Ring
40. Standing Dreidel
41. Clay Dreidels
42. Newspaper Wrapping Paper
43. Folded and Dipped Wrapping Paper
44. Macaroni Star
45. Textured Wine Bottle
46. Label for Wine Decanter
47. Melted Crayon Bookcovers

679
B

Becker, Joyce.
Hanukkah crafts

MAY 10 '79	DATE DUE		
DEC 3 '79			
DEC 20 '79			
DEC 2 '80			
DEC 16			
JAN 8 '85			
FEB 17 '85			
DEC 13 '85			

BETH HILLEL LIBRARY
WILMETTE, ILLINOIS

WITHDRAWN